The Body
Project

Programs *That Work*™

Editor-in-Chief

David H. Barlow, PhD

Scientific Advisory Board

Anne Marie Albano, PhD

Jack M. Gorman, MD

Peter E. Nathan, PhD

Bonnie Spring, PhD

Paul Salkovskis, PhD

John R. Weisz, PhD

G. Terence Wilson, PhD

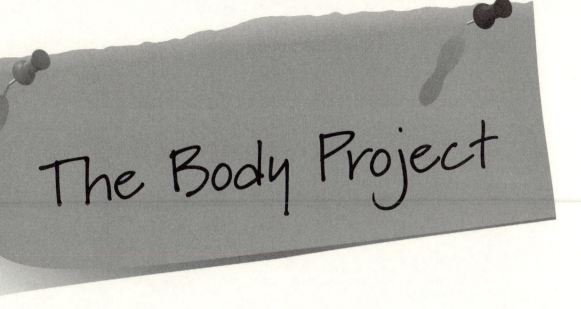

The Body Project

Promoting Body Acceptance and Preventing Eating Disorders

Facilitator Guide

Eric Stice • Katherine Presnell

OXFORD
UNIVERSITY PRESS

2007

OXFORD
UNIVERSITY PRESS

Oxford University Press, Inc., publishes works that further
Oxford University's objective of excellence
in research, scholarship, and education.

Oxford   New York
Auckland   Cape Town   Dar es Salaam   Hong Kong   Karachi
Kuala Lumpur   Madrid   Melbourne   Mexico City   Nairobi
New Delhi   Shanghai   Taipei   Toronto

With offices in
Argentina   Austria   Brazil   Chile   Czech Republic   France   Greece
Guatemala   Hungary   Italy   Japan   Poland   Portugal   Singapore
South Korea   Switzerland   Thailand   Turkey   Ukraine   Vietnam

Published by Oxford University Press, Inc.
198 Madison Avenue, New York, New York 10016

www.oup.com

Oxford is a registered trademark of Oxford University Press

Library of Congress Cataloging-in-Publication Data
Stice, Eric.
The body project : promoting body acceptance and preventing eating
disorders : facilitator guide /
Eric Stice and Katherine Presnell.
p.   cm.
Includes bibliographical references.
ISBN 978-0-19-531989-7 (pbk.)
1. Body image disturbance—Treatment.   2. Eating disorders—Prevention.
I. Presnell, Katherine.   II. Title.   III. Series: Treatments that work.
[DNLM: 1. Body Image.   2. Self Concept.   3. Eating Disorders—prevention &
control.   4. Psychotherapy, Group—methods. WM 190 S854b 2007]
RC569.5.B65S75 2007
616.85'26—dc22   2006030674

9 8 7 6 5 4 3 2 1

Printed in the United States of America
on acid-free paper

Stunning developments in healthcare have taken place over the last several years, but many of our widely accepted interventions and strategies in mental health and behavioral medicine have been brought into question by research demonstrating not only lack of benefit, but perhaps induction of harm. Other strategies have been proven effective using the best current standards of evidence, resulting in broad-based recommendations to make these practices more available to the public. Several recent developments are behind this revolution. First, we have arrived at a much deeper understanding of pathology, both psychological and physical, which has led to the development of new, more precisely targeted interventions. Second, our research methodologies have improved substantially, such that we have reduced threats to internal and external validity, making the outcomes more directly applicable to clinical situations. Third, governments around the world and healthcare systems and policymakers have decided that the quality of care should improve, that it should be evidence based, and that it is in the public's interest to ensure that this happens (Barlow, 2004; Institute of Medicine, 2001).

Of course, the major stumbling block for clinicians everywhere is the accessibility of newly developed, evidence-based psychological interventions. Workshops and books can go only so far in acquainting responsible and conscientious practitioners with the latest behavioral healthcare practices and their applicability to individual patients. This new series, Programs *ThatWork*™, is devoted to communicating these exciting new interventions to clinicians on the frontlines of practice.

The manuals and workbooks in this series contain detailed step-by-step procedures for assessing and treating specific problems and diagnoses. But this series also goes beyond the books and manuals by providing ancillary materials that will fulfill a "supervisory" role in guiding practitioners in implementing these procedures in their practice.

In our continually evolving healthcare system, the growing consensus is that evidence-based practice offers the most responsible course of action for the mental health professional. All behavioral healthcare clinicians deeply desire to provide the best possible care for their patients. In this series, our aim is to close the dissemination and information gap and make that possible.

This facilitator's guide is the first manual in the new branch of the successful Treatments *ThatWork*™ series called Programs *ThatWork*™. Statistics show that 90% of the millions of Americans diagnosed with eating disorders annually are adolescent and young women. This prevention program was designed with them in mind.

The Body Project is a cognitive-dissonance–based body-acceptance intervention for use in group therapy. This time-limited group treatment has proven effective in helping adolescent girls and young women resist sociocultural pressures to conform to the thin ideal and reduce their pursuit of thinness. The result of 16 years of research, the Body Project has been found to reduce thin-ideal internalization, body dissatisfaction, negative mood, unhealthy dieting, and eating disorder symptoms in adolescent girls and young women with body image concerns. This intervention has also been found to reduce the risk for future onset of eating disorder symptoms.

This book is a welcome addition to our growing list of psychological treatments and interventions with empirical support and can be delivered by real-world providers such as school counselors, nurses, and teachers, in addition to skilled clinicians. It is an accessible treatment with a proven success rate.

David H. Barlow, Editor-in-Chief

Programs *ThatWork*™

Boston, Massachusetts

Contents

The Body Project

Part
1

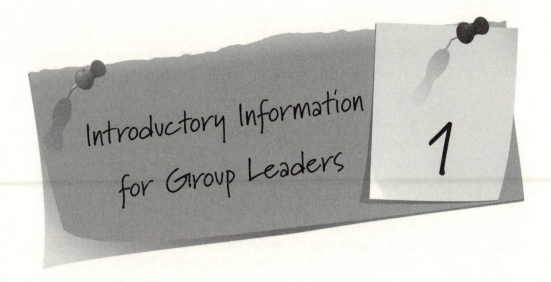

Introductory Information
for Group Leaders

1

Background Information and Purpose of This Program

In Western culture, appearance is a central evaluative dimension for females, and the current ideal favors an ultrathin figure. Thin-ideal internalization, or the degree to which one subscribes to this socially defined ideal of attractiveness and engages in behaviors aimed at achieving this look, theoretically fosters a sense of dissatisfaction with one's body because this ideal is extremely difficult to attain.

The Body Project is a cognitive-dissonance–based body-acceptance intervention that was designed to help adolescent girls and young women resist sociocultural pressures to conform to this ideal and reduce their pursuit of thinness. A reduction in thin-ideal internalization should result in improved body satisfaction and improved mood, reduced use of unhealthy weight-control behaviors, and decreased binge eating and other eating disorder symptoms. Consistent with this expectation, randomized prevention trials conducted by at least five independent labs have found that the Body Project eating disorder prevention program reduces thin-ideal internalization, body dissatisfaction, negative mood, unhealthy dieting, and eating disorder symptoms. This intervention has also been found to reduce risk for future onset of eating disorder symptoms. In addition, there is evidence that the Body Project intervention reduces risk for future onset of obesity, results in improved psychosocial functioning, and reduces mental health care utilization. Research trials conducted by independent labs have found that the Body Project significantly outperforms alternative interventions and that it remains effective when delivered by providers such as school counselors, nurses, and teachers.

Although the Body Project was originally designed for use with adolescent girls and young women with body image concerns, who are at high-risk for development of eating problems, research has shown that the program is effective for non–high-risk populations of female students in high school and college as well. To the best of our knowledge, no other eating disorder prevention program that has been evaluated to date has yielded significant intervention effects for this wide range of clinically important outcomes across so many independent labs.

The conceptual basis for the Body Project is that if girls and young women voluntarily argue against the thin ideal, this will result in a reduced subscription to this ideal and to consequent decreases in eating disorder risk factors and eating-disordered behaviors. Thus, this intervention involves a series of verbal, written, and behavioral exercises in which the students critique the thin ideal. Theoretically, the act of publicly critiquing the thin ideal results in cognitive dissonance among those who originally endorsed this ideal, which causes them to reduce their subscription to the thin ideal. As such, the Body Project intervention attempts to apply persuasion principles, originally identified by social psychologists, to reduce an attitudinal risk factor for eating pathology. All exercises are focused solely on providing an opportunity for the participants to critique the thin ideal; no other risk factors are expressly targeted in this intervention. It is paramount that the participants, rather than the group leaders, critique the thin ideal, because participants will not experience dissonance if group leaders do the critiquing. This intervention also strives to minimize didactic presentation of psychoeducational material by the group leader because research has suggested that the didactic strategy does not reduce risk for current or future eating pathology.

The Body Project intervention was originally developed and used at Stanford University, but it was further refined and evaluated at the University of Texas at Austin and in high schools in Austin, Texas, and Eugene, Oregon. The intervention is the outgrowth of a 16-year program of research. In this program of research we first conducted a series of prospective studies to identify risk factors that predict the onset of eating pathology. We then systematically began to develop and evaluate prevention programs to reduce the risk factors for which there were the greatest empirical support. To our knowledge, ours is one of the few eating disorder prevention programs based on a generative program of research. Independent labs at Trinity University in San Antonio Texas, Trinity College, Hartford Connecticut, Yale University, University of South Florida, and Iowa State University have also evaluated versions of this prevention program and contributed to the evidence base for this intervention. At the time this manual went to press, more than 1000 adolescent girls and young women have completed this program.

Problem Focus

The primary objective of the Body Project intervention is to reduce risk for current and future eating pathology and eating disorder symptoms. We use the term "eating pathology" to refer to threshold and subthreshold anorexia nervosa, bulimia nervosa, and binge-eating disorder. In the following sections we list the *Diagnostic and Statistical Manual of Mental Disorders, fourth edition, text revision (DSM-IV-TR;* APA, 2000) criteria for each of the eating disorders. Individuals who exhibit these symptoms but who are below diagnostic threshold on one or more criteria would typically be considered to meet subthreshold criteria for that eating disorder (e.g., individuals who report the use of binge eating and compensatory behaviors on average only once a week).

Diagnostic Criteria for Anorexia Nervosa

Below are the diagnostic criteria for anorexia nervosa according to the *DSM-IV-TR* (APA, 2000):

A. Refusal to maintain body weight at or above a minimally normal weight for age and height (e.g., weight loss leading to maintenance of body weight less than 85% of that expected, or failure to make expected weight gain during periods of growth, leading to body weight less than 85% of that expected).

B. Intense fear of gaining weight or becoming fat, even though underweight.

C. Disturbance in the way in which one's body weight or shape is experienced, undue influence of body weight or shape on one's self-evaluation, or denial of the seriousness of the current low body weight.

D. In postmenarcheal females, amenorrhea (i.e., the absence of at least three consecutive menstrual cycles). A woman is considered to have amenorrhea if her periods occur only after hormone administration.

Diagnostic Criteria for Bulimia Nervosa

Belows are the diagnostic criteria for bulimia nervosa according to the *DSM-IV-TR* (APA, 2000).

A. Recurrent episodes of binge eating. An episode of binge eating is characterized by:
   1. Eating, in a discrete period of time (e.g., within any 2-hour period), an amount of food that is larger than most people would eat during a similar period of time and under similar circumstances
   2. A sense of lack of control over eating during the episode (e.g., a feeling that one cannot stop eating or control what or how much one is eating).

B. Recurrent, inappropriate compensatory behavior in order to prevent weight gain, such as self-induced vomiting; misuse of laxatives, diuretics, enemas, or other medications; fasting; or excessive exercise.

C. The binge eating and inappropriate compensatory behaviors both occur, on average, at least twice a week for 3 months.

D. Self-evaluation is unduly influenced by body shape and weight.

E. The disturbance does not occur exclusively during episodes of anorexia nervosa.

Diagnostic Criteria for Binge-Eating Disorder

Below are the diagnostic criteria for binge-eating disorder according to the *DSM-IV-TR* (APA, 2000).

A. Recurrent episodes of binge eating. An episode of binge eating is characterized by:
   1. Eating, in a discrete period of time (e.g., within any 2-hour period), an amount of food that is larger than most people would eat during a similar period of time and under similar circumstances
   2. A sense of lack of control over eating during the episode (e.g., a feeling that one cannot stop eating or control what or how much one is eating).

B. The binge-eating episodes are associated with three (or more) of the following:
   1. Eating much more rapidly than normal
   2. Eating until feeling uncomfortably full
   3. Eating large amounts of food when not feeling physically hungry
   4. Eating alone because of being embarrassed by how much one is eating
   5. Feeling disgusted with oneself, depressed, or very guilty after overeating.

C. Marked distress regarding binge-eating is present.

D. The binge eating occurs, on average, at least 2 days a week for 6 months.

E. The binge eating is not associated with the regular use of inappropriate compensatory behaviors (e.g., purging, fasting, excessive exercise) and does not occur exclusively during the course of anorexia nervosa or bulimia nervosa.

Threshold and subthreshold eating disorders are one of the most prevalent classes of psychiatric disorders for adolescent and young adult females. Community-recruited epidemiology studies indicate that the lifetime rates among girls and young women is 1.4%–2.0% for anorexia nervosa, 1.1%–3.0% for subthreshold anorexia nervosa, 1.1%–4.6% for bulimia nervosa, 2.0%–5.4% for subthreshold bulimia nervosa, 0.2%–1.5% for binge-eating disorder, and approximately 1.6% for subthreshold binge-eating disorder (Favaro, Ferrara, & Santonastaso, 2003; Hoek & van Hoeken, 2003; Kjelsas, Bjornstrom, & Gotestam, 2004; Lewinsohn, Hops, Roberts, Seeley, & Andrews, 1993; Lewinsohn, Striegel-Moore, & Seeley, 2000; Woodside et al., 2001).

The course and outcome of anorexia nervosa are highly variable: some individuals recover after a brief period of illness, some oscillate between marked weight loss and hospitalization and periods of restoration of normal weight, some show weight restoration but experience some other eating disorder, and some never recover from this eating disorder (Wilson, Becker, & Heffernan, 2003). Analysis of samples of community-recruited subjects suggest that bulimia nervosa typically shows a chronic course characterized by periods of recovery, relapse, and diagnostic transitions to other eating disorder variants, whereas subthreshold bulimic pathology shows less chronicity (Bohon, Muscatell, Burton, & Stice, 2005; Grilo et al., 2003; Fairburn, Cooper, Doll, Norman, & O'Connor, 2000). Community-recruited natural history studies suggest that binge-eating disorder often shows a high remission rate over time, with nearly 50% of patients showing recovery by 6-month follow-up (Cachelin, Striegel-Moore, Elder, Pike, Wilfley, & Fairburn, 1999) and approximately 80% of patients showing recovery by 3- to 5-year follow-up (Fairburn et al., 2000; Wilson et al., 2003). However, some studies found that many individuals with binge-eating disorder developed EDNOS (eating disorder—not otherwise specified) or continued to show some residual symptoms (Fairburn et al., 2000). Even with the current treatments of choice, most individuals with anorexia nervosa, bulimia nervosa, and binge-eating disorder rarely make a full recovery from these disorders, which persist over a multi-year follow-up (e.g., Agras, Walsh, Fairburn, Wilson, & Kraemer, 2000; Strober, Freeman, & Morrell, 1997; Wilfley et al., 2002).

Preventing the development of eating disorders is an important goal because these disorders contribute to a wide variety of adverse outcomes. Eating disorders, particularly anorexia nervosa, have been found to increase risk for mortality (Keel et al., 2003; Wilson et al., 2003). Prospective studies have also found that threshold and subthreshold bulimia nervosa increase the risk for future onset of depression, suicide attempts, anxiety disorders, substance abuse, and obesity and other health problems (Johnson, Cohen, Kasen, & Brook, 2002; Stice, Cameron, Killen, Hayward, & Taylor, 1999; Stice, Hayward, Cameron, Killen, & Taylor, 2000; Striegel-Moore, Seeley, & Lewinsohn, 2003). Another study revealed that individuals with binge-eating disorder show high rates of obesity in the future (Fairburn et al., 2000). Moreover, because only 25%–50% of individuals with eating disorders ever seek treatment (Johnson et al., 2002; Newman et al., 1996) and only 30%–50% of patients receiving treatment show lasting symptom remission (Agras et al., 2000; Wilfley et al., 2002), preventing these pernicious disorders is especially important.

The secondary objective of the Body Project intervention is to reduce empirically established risk factors for eating pathology, including thin-ideal internalization, body dissatisfaction, unhealthy dieting, and negative affect. The intervention uses dissonance-induction procedures that focus expressly on reducing thin-ideal internalization, a risk factor hypothesized to occur early in the causal chain. According to the dual pathway model that has guided our program of research (Stice, 2001), a reduction in thin-ideal internalization results in a reduction in body dissatisfaction, negative affect, and unhealthy weight control behaviors. It is desirable to reduce several of these risk factors, particularly body dissatisfaction and negative affect, because they produce significant distress and impairment, and they contribute to eating pathology. Body dissatisfaction is associated with negative affect, preoccupation with appearance, and unnecessary cosmetic surgery (Thompson, Heinberg, Altabe, & Tantleff-Dunn, 1999). Negative affect is associated with academic difficulties, interpersonal problems, substance abuse, impaired social functioning, and suicidal ideation (Capaldi & Stoolmiller, 1999; Gotlib, Lewinsohn, & Seeley, 1998; Lewinsohn, Solomon, Seeley, & Zeiss, 2000; Nolen-Hoeksema, Girgus, & Seligman, 1992).

Reducing risk factors for the onset of obesity is important because obesity is currently credited with more than 100,000 deaths annually in the United States (Flegal, Graubard, Williamson, & Gail, 2005). In addition, obesity is associated with serious medical problems, including high blood pressure, unhealthy lipoprotein profiles, diabetes mellitus, atherosclerotic cerebrovascular disease, coronary heart disease, and colorectal cancer, as well as lower educational attainment and higher rates of poverty (Dietz, 2004; Pietrobelli et al., 1998). Currently, approximately 65% of adults are overweight or obese, which represents a dramatic increase over the last several decades (Hedley et al., 2004). The prevalence of obesity has risen even more sharply during this time among adolescents and young adults (Hedley et al., 2004; Ogden, Flegal, Carroll, & Johnson, 2002), which is troubling because approximately 70% of obese adolescents will become obese adults (Magarey, Daniels, Boulton, & Cockington, 2003).

Development of This Prevention Intervention and Evidence Base

Historically, eating disorder prevention programs have primarily focused on providing information about the adverse effects of eating disorders, with the hope that this will reduce the rates of these disorders. Psychoeducational programs, however, have met with limited success in preventing eating disorders (see Stice & Shaw, 2004) and obesity (Stice, Shaw, & Marti, 2006), which is not surprising given that these types of interventions have not been successful in preventing other problems, including substance abuse, depression, and unprotected sexual intercourse (e.g., Clarke, Hawkins, Murphy, & Sheeber, 1993; Larimer & Cronce, 2002; Mann, Tarantola, & Netter, 1992).

These findings suggested the need to develop alternative approaches to preventing eating disorders. We attempted to create a new approach for producing attitudinal and behavioral change. One approach that appeared promising was a cognitive dissonance-based intervention. Cognitive dissonance theory, which is an outgrowth of social psychological principles, proposes that having inconsistent cognitions creates psychological discomfort that motivates people to alter their beliefs to produce greater consistency (Festinger, 1957). This phenomenon has been demonstrated in numerous induced compliance experiments, where participants who take a counter-attitudinal stance experience cognitive dissonance, which leads to an attitudinal shift toward the new perspective, thereby reducing the inconsistency (Leippe, 1994). If the participants do not feel that the attitudinal shift was voluntary, the inconsistent position is attributed to situational demands, and no attitudinal change results. Laboratory experiments have also demonstrated that more effortful expression of

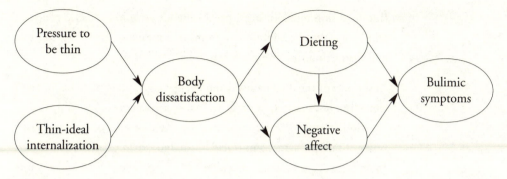

Figure 1.1

Theoretical components of the dual pathway model of bulimic pathology.

the alternative viewpoint and expression of this viewpoint in a public, versus a private, setting also increase the degree of dissonance induction (Green, Scott, Diyankova, Gasser, & Pederson, 2005). Because a dissonance approach effectively produced attitudinal change in laboratory experiments, we decided to adapt this technique for eating disorder prevention.

The Body Project intervention is based on the general framework of the dual pathway model of bulimia nervosa (Stice, 2001). This etiologic model posits that internalization of the thin ideal espoused for women contributes to body dissatisfaction because this ideal is virtually unattainable (see figure 1.1). The model also hypothesizes that elevated pressure to be thin from family, peers, and the media fosters body dissatisfaction, as repeated messages that one is not thin enough likely promotes discontent with one's body. Theoretically, this increased body dissatisfaction in turn fosters dieting and negative affect, which consequently increase the risk for bulimic pathology. Body dissatisfaction is thought to lead to dieting because of the common belief that dieting is an effective weight control technique. Body dissatisfaction may also contribute to negative affect because appearance is a central evaluative dimension for women in our culture. Dieting is thought to foster negative affect because of the failures that are often associated with weight control efforts and the impact of caloric deprivation on mood. Dieting is also theorized to result in a greater risk for bulimic pathology because individuals may binge to counteract the effects of caloric deprivation. Further, dieting might promote binge eating because breaking strict dietary rules can result in disinhibited eating (the abstinence-violation effect). Negative affect might foster bulimic symptoms as a means of providing comfort and distraction from negative emotions.

In support of the dual pathway model, perceived pressure to be thin and thin-ideal internalization predicted subsequent increases in body dissatisfaction (Cattarin & Thompson, 1994; Field et al., 2001; Stice, 2001), onset of bulimic symptoms (Field, Camargo, Taylor, Berkey, & Colditz, 1999; Stice & Agras, 1998; Stice, Presnell, & Spangler, 2002) and any eating disorder (threshold or subthreshold bulimia nervosa, anorexia nervosa, or binge eating disorder; McKnight Investigators, 2003). Moreover, body dissatisfaction predicted future increases in dieting and negative affect (Cooley & Toray, 2001; Stice, 2001; Wertheim, Koerner, & Paxton, 2001), increases in bulimic symptoms (Cooley & Toray, 2001; Stice, 2001), onset of bulimic symptoms (Field et al., 1999; Stice & Agras, 1998; Stice et al., 2002), and onset of bulimic pathology (Killen et al., 1994, 1996). Dieting and negative affect predicted future increases in bulimic symptoms (Cooley & Toray, 2001; Stice, 2001), onset of bulimic symptoms (Field et al., 1999; Stice & Agras, 1998; Stice et al., 2002), and onset of bulimic pathology (Killen et al., 1993, 1996). Perhaps more important, experimental psychopathology trials with young women that have decreased the risk factors in this model, including thin-ideal internalization, body dissatisfaction, and negative affect, resulted in subsequent decreases in bulimic pathology (Bearman, Stice, & Chase, 2003; Burton, Stice, Bearman, & Rohde, in press; Stice, Mazotti, Weibel, & Agras, 2000). The one exception is that individuals who are randomly assigned to low-calorie diets show decreased, rather than the hypothesized increased, bulimic symptoms relative to waitlist controls (Burton & Stice, 2006; Groesz & Stice, 2007; Presnell & Stice, 2003). It appears that the conflicting findings regarding dieting arose because self-report dietary restraint scales used in the prospective studies are not valid measures of actual caloric restriction (Bathalon et al., 2000; Martin et al., 2005; Stice, Fisher, & Lowe, 2004; Sysko, Walsh, Schebendach, & Wilson 2005).

The Body Project intervention thus encourages adolescent girls and young women who subscribe to the thin ideal to voluntarily critique it through a series of verbal, written, and behavioral exercises. These activities are theorized to produce cognitive dissonance, which is resolved by reducing the intensity of an individual's belief in the thin ideal, resulting in reduced body dissatisfaction, negative affect, ineffective dieting, and eating disorder symptoms. This intervention can also be thought of as a form of strategic self-presentation (Leake, Friend, & Wadhwa, 1999; Stone, Aronson, Craing, Winslow, & Fried, 1994), which attempts to promote adaptive behavior by having participants model such behavior in a group setting. Several exercises in the dissonance intervention can also be viewed from a cognitive-behavioral perspective as providing an opportunity to disconfirm maladaptive cognitions that maintain body dissatisfaction (Roehrig, Thompson, Brannick, & van den Berg, 2006).

Several general principles guided the development of the Body Project. First, we minimized didactic presentation because this type of intervention appears to be less effective than interactive techniques (Stice & Shaw, 2004). Second, to facilitate skill acquisition, we included in-session exercises that require participants to apply the skills taught in the intervention. Third, between-session homework was used to help participants learn how to apply these skills in the real world. Fourth, we used motivational enhancement exercises (Miller, 1983) to maximize a participant's incentive to use the new skills (e.g., reviewing the costs of body image concerns as a group). Fifth, we included group activities to foster social support and group cohesion.

Note that because selective prevention programs have been found to be significantly more effective than universal programs in preventing eating disorders (Stice & Shaw, 2004), females considered to be at high risk of developing eating disorders due to elevated body image concerns have generally been targeted for the intervention. Thus, recruitment materials usually described the study as a body acceptance program for girls and young women with body image concerns. As mentioned earlier, other studies have shown that the Body Project intervention produces positive effects for adolescent girls and young women who are not at elevated risk for eating pathology. Participants are not made aware of the expectation that the intervention will reduce or prevent eating pathology, which minimizes demand characteristics for effects on this outcome. Participants are typically recruited through a combination of the following methods: flyers, e-mails, mailings, school and local newspapers, school web pages, and class announcements. We have found that the use of flyers with pictures of women from a wide variety of ethnic groups assists in the recruitment of members from other minority groups. As discussed below, this intervention was designed for delivery by trained professionals, including school nurses, school counselors, social workers, psychologists, and psychiatrists, although there is also emerging evidence that it can be delivered effectively by school teachers.

It is also important to note that the development of this program has been iterative. Information gleaned from randomized trials is used to improve and refine the program for the next evaluation (Coie et al., 1993). Accordingly, qualitative input from participants and group leaders who have participated in each trial has been collected and used to improve the subsequent version of this intervention for the next trial.

Outline of This Program

Structure

All of the studies evaluating this program (see "Evaluations of This Intervention," below) have been conducted in a group format, rather than in an individual format. This serves several purposes, including capitalizing on social cohesion among group members, promoting attitude change by hearing other peers express statements against the thin ideal, and maximizing cost effectiveness. The group leader can be a school counselor, psychologist, nurse, or teacher. It is often useful to include a coleader, who may have participated in a previous group, to help conduct the sessions (e.g., pass out materials and write participant responses on a whiteboard). Experience suggests that the optimal group size is approximately six to eight participants because this ensures that all group members will be able to participate verbally and that group leaders will allocate sufficient attention to each individual participant for in-session exercises.

The program is designed to be presented in four 1-hour sessions conducted over 4 consecutive weeks, and our clinical experience suggests that conducting the sessions one week apart helps the participants learn and practice the skills discussed in-session. However, as we discussed later in this chapter, positive effects have been obtained when the program has been delivered in a shorter, more condensed period, although the effects tend to be somewhat weaker. Each session begins with a review of skills or concepts discussed in previous sessions and thus builds on the previous session. Group leaders should explain the rationale for each of the exercises presented in session and at home and strongly encourage participants to read and complete the assigned exercises between sessions. It is crucial that group leaders manage the session effectively and make sure that all listed exercises are completed. It is sometimes necessary to tactfully interrupt particularly talkative individuals so that the group leader can move the group to the next exercise.

Group Leader Training

This manual has been developed for school counselors, psychologists, nurses, or teachers. In our research program, psychologists and doctoral students in clinical psychology have generally served as group leaders, but the Body Project intervention has been successfully implemented by a variety of individuals with varying levels of clinical training. The ideal group leader conducting this program would be familiar with dissonance theory, have an understanding of the sociocultural pressures to be thin facing women in our culture, and possess basic therapeutic and empathy skills. It is vital for group leaders to carefully read this manual and practice each activity (i.e., role play) before attempting to lead a group. Participants quickly lose interest if the group leaders are not familiar with the activities and the flow of the sessions.

Common Problems

Missed Sessions

If a participant misses a session, try to schedule a 15-minute mini-session with the student to cover the important points and exercises before they attend the next scheduled session. This can be done just before the next session begins. Although this represents extra work for the group leaders, it minimizes missed sessions and lets each participant know that she is important.

At-Home Exercises

Home exercises can pose difficulties, especially those that seem "school-like." How well participants complete between-session assignments depends on whether leaders emphasize the importance of completing the exercises and how well they track students' performance of the exercises. Contacting participants via email or phone a day before the scheduled session prompts participants to complete their assignments and bring them to their next session. It is also useful to ask participants to explain the at-home exercises back to you after you've explained them to make sure that they understand the exercises.

Investment in the Thin-Ideal

Participants often are extremely invested in the thin ideal at the outset and have difficulty letting go of this pursuit. However, it is important not to allow participants to argue for the thin ideal, as this will only further solidify their position. Additionally, you should refrain from arguing with group members or attempting to persuade group members that they should not pursue the thin ideal. Always keep in mind that the primary goal of the intervention is to get the *participants* to criticize and challenge the thin ideal. Group leaders should try to get other group members to speak out against the thin ideal or pose counter arguments to pro–thin-ideal statements voiced by participants. The program does not work if *participants* do not critique the thin ideal. It is also important that you keep self-disclosure regarding personal experiences (including a history of eating problems) or attitudes to a minimum, to make sure that participants can maximize the time spend critiquing the thin ideal.

Thin Ideal vs. Healthy Ideal

It is important to make a distinction between the thin ideal and the healthy ideal. The thin ideal involves appearing ultraslender, whatever the cost. People may be willing to engage in very unhealthy behaviors to attain this slenderness, including laxative abuse, and extreme behaviors, such as cosmetic surgery, to attain this look. In contrast, the healthy ideal involves striving for a healthy body, which is typically not nearly as slender as the thin ideal, in part because it is healthy to have strong muscles. Further, individuals pursuing the healthy ideal do not engage in unhealthy weight control behaviors, such as fasting and laxative abuse.

Participant Engagement

It is also important to actively engage all participants during the group sessions. Although it is crucial to follow the manual closely, participants often get bored if group leaders read directly from the script. Thus, we recommend that you become familiar with the main points to minimize in-session reliance on the script. Maintaining eye contact with participants during the entire session also helps encourage discussion. Be sure to look at each participant and try to draw her into the discussions, paying special attention to those who are less talkative or reluctant to speak up. If one or two participants tend to dominate the discussion, call on other participants to share their opinions. We recommend systematically going around the entire group so that each group member participates in each main activity (change the order so the same person does not always have to go first). In general, we have found that using humor when possible, appearing relaxed, smiling and laughing when appropriate, and listening carefully to what participants are saying helps draw participants in. When a participant shares personal information or discusses the difficulties they have with body image, it is appropriate and desirable to make empathetic statements ("Wow, it sounds like you're really struggling with this"; "That must have been hurtful when your father made that comment to you about your weight"). Although it is extremely important to stay on track and cover the necessary information for each session, participants should feel that they have been heard and understood.

Outline of This Intervention

This prevention intervention consists of four sessions that involve written, verbal, and behavioral exercises designed to induce cognitive dissonance regarding pursuit of the thin ideal.

Session 1

The focus of session 1 is on providing an overview of the purpose of the study and introducing participants to the rules and expectations of the group. Participants are informed that this intervention is based on the idea that a discussion of how to help younger girls avoid body image problems can help them improve their own body satisfaction. This first session then covers the following:

■ Verbally affirming each participants' willingness and commitment to try this approach

■ Discussing the definition and origins of the thin ideal

■ Exploring how the thin ideal is perpetuated, the impact of messages about the thin ideal from family, peers, dating partners, and the media, and how corporations profit from this ideal

■ Explaining home exercises and two specific exercises to be completed before the next session.

Session 2

Session 2 begins with a review of the materials discussed in the previous session and a discussion of participants' experiences of and reactions to the first-session exercises. In-session exercises are used to help participants voluntarily take a counter-attitudinal stance. Specific exercises in this session include:

■ Discussing a self-affirmation mirror exercise and the feelings and thoughts surrounding the completion of this home exercise

■ Introducing role plays with participants to elicit verbal statements against the thin ideal

■ Explaining home exercises, including identifying personal examples concerning pressures to be thin that participants have encountered and generating verbal challenges to these pressures, and producing a list of things girls/women can do to resist the thin ideal (e.g., what can they avoid, say, do, or learn to battle this ideal)

■ Reminding participants to bring the two home exercise forms to the next session for discussion.

Session 3

The third session with a review of the materials discussed in the previous session and a discussion of participants' experiences of and reactions to the second-session exercises. In session 3 the group leader continues to reinforce counter-attitudinal statements with role plays and introduces behavioral exercises. Specific exercises in this session include:

■ Discussing personal examples concerning pressure to be thin and elicitation of verbal challenges to these pressures

■ Performing role plays of counter thin-ideal statements to resist pressure to be thin from peers

■ Discussing the reasons participants signed up for the class and identification of individual body-related concerns

■ Challenging participants to engage in a behavioral experiment relating to personal body image concerns in the following week as a home exercise

■ Discussing previous home exercise regarding list of things girls/women can do to resist the thin ideal

■ Assigning a second home exercise to enact one activism behavior during the next week

■ Reminding participants to bring the two home exercise forms to the next session for discussion.

Session 4

After reviewing the main points from the last session, the fourth session focuses on examining nuances of the thin ideal and discussing future pressures to be thin. This session includes the following components:

■ Sharing each participants' experiences with the behavioral challenge and her reactions to this exercise

- Encouraging participants to continue challenging themselves and their body-related concerns in the future

- Discussing participants' experiences with the body activism exercise

- Examining more subtle ways in which the thin ideal often gets perpetuated (e.g., complimenting a friend on weight loss, joining in when friends complain about their bodies)

- Identifying these types of subtle statements from a list and explaining how each perpetuates the thin ideal

- Exploring difficulties participants might encounter in resisting the thin ideal and how each could be addressed

- Discussing future pressures to conform to the thin ideal that participants are likely to face in the future and ways of dealing with those pressures

- Discussing how to talk about one's body in a positive, rather than a negative, way

- Explaining and assigning two exit exercises to be completed over the following week, including one written exercise and one self-affirmation exercise.

Assessment

You may want to monitor improvement from pre- to posttreatment in order to evaluate the success of the intervention in reducing or preventing onset of eating disorder symptoms and reducing risk factors for eating disorders. Posttreatment self-report instruments can be used to identify patients who have symptoms such as residual affective problems that indicate that they need clinical attention. We have used several different scales in our research studies to examine the Body Project intervention.

The Eating Disorder Diagnostic Scale (EDDS; Stice, Telch, & Rizvi, 2000) is a brief self-report scale assessing *DSM-IV-TR* criteria for anorexia nervosa, bulimia nervosa, and binge-eating disorder. This scale generates diagnoses for all three eating disorders, as well as a continuous eating disorder symptom composite. The EDDS has shown high agreement (κ = .78–.83) with eating disorder diagnoses made with the Eating Disorder Examination (EDE; Fairburn & Cooper, 1993), internal consistency (α = .89), 1-week test–retest reliability (r = .87), sensitivity to detecting intervention effects, and predictive validity for future onset of eating pathology and depression (Stice, Fisher, & Martinez, 2004; Stice, Telch, & Rizvi, 2000).

To assess risk factors for eating disorders, we have used the eight-item Ideal-Body Stereotype Scale-Revised, which assesses thin-ideal internalization (Stice, Fisher et al., 2004). Items use a response format ranging from 1 = *strongly disagree* to 5 = *strongly agree* and are averaged for this scale. This scale has shown internal consistency (α = .91), test–retest reliability (r = .80), and predictive validity for bulimic symptom onset (Stice, Fisher et al., 2004). In the context of assessing risk factors, we have also used the Satisfaction and Dissatisfaction with Body Parts Scale (Berscheid, Walster, & Bohrnstedt, 1973). Participants indicate their level of satisfaction with body parts (e.g., stomach and hips) on scales ranging from 1 = *extremely satisfied* to 6 = *extremely dissatisfied*. This scale has shown internal consistency (α = .94), 3-week test–retest reliability (r = .90), and predictive validity for bulimic symptom onset (Stice, Fisher et al., 2004).

Another scale we have used to assess risk factors is the 10-item Dutch Restrained Eating Scale, which assesses dieting (DRES; van Strien, Frijters, van Staveren, Defares, & Deurenberg, 1986). Participants indicate the frequency of dieting behaviors using scales ranging from 1 = *never* to 5 = *always*. The DRES has shown internal consistency (α = .95), 2-week test–retest reliability (r = .82), convergent validity with self-reported caloric intake (though it shows weaker relations to objectively measured intake), and predictive validity for bulimic symptom onset (Stice, Fisher et al., 2004; van Strien et al., 1986). Finally, negative affect can be assessed with the sadness, guilt, and fear/anxiety subscales from the Positive Affect and Negative Affect Scale-Revised (Watson & Clark, 1992). Participants report how much they have felt various negative emotional states on scales ranging from 1 = *very slightly or not at all* to 5 = *extremely*. This scale has shown internal consistency (α = .95), 3-week test-retest reliability (r = .78), convergent validity, and predictive validity for bulimic symptom onset (Stice, Trost, & Chase, 2003; Watson & Clark, 1992).

Use of The Workbook

Group leaders using this program should first read the corresponding workbook and become familiar with the basic structure and exercises of each session. The Group Leader's Guide presents supplemental background information on the theory and research on which this program is based and provides suggestions on how to deal with challenges that may arise during the sessions. The workbook was developed for group members to use to complete at-home exercises, as well as to reinforce information presented in the sessions. Participants will be able to consult this workbook between scheduled sessions, clarify any confusion regarding homework assignments, share information with friends and family members, and refer back to the workbook once the program is completed.

Evaluations of This Intervention

The Body Project program has received empirical support in 12 controlled trials conducted by 5 independent labs. Nine of these trials were efficacy studies evaluating the impact of the Body Project intervention program when research staff actively recruited participants and trained professionals delivered the intervention (typically Ph.D.-level psychologists or graduate students). These trials evaluated the initial three 1-hour session version of this intervention. Several researchers have also conducted effectiveness trials that tested whether the program produces positive outcomes when school personnel, such as counselors, nurses, and teachers, are responsible for recruitment and intervention delivery. Effectiveness trials are particularly important because they test whether the intervention produces positive effects when delivered in an ecologically valid way by real-world providers (Hoagwood, Hibbs, Brent, & Jensen, 1995). The effectiveness trials have typically evaluated expanded 4-hour versions of this intervention, delivered in four 1-hour sessions or in two 2-hour sessions, with the goal of making it easier for school-based interventionists to adequately cover all the material. Available trials evaluating the Body Project intervention are reviewed below.

Efficacy Trial 1

In the first preliminary trial, 30 high-risk young women (M age $=$ 18) with elevated body image concerns were assigned to a three-session Body Project program or a waitlist control condition (Stice, Mazotti et al., 2000). We were unable to randomly assign participants to condition in this first trial because of scheduling constraints. In this trial, and in all others conducted by our research group, we allowed adolescent girls and young women to self-select into the program if they felt that had body image concerns; we did not use a specific screener to identify those with body image concerns because it seemed unnecessary. Compared with controls, program participants showed significantly greater decreases in thin-ideal internalization, body dissatisfaction, negative affect, and bulimic symptoms, but not in dietary restraint scores, from pretest to posttest. All effects, except for negative affect, remained significant through the 1-month follow-up. It was noteworthy that the intervention appeared to prevent the significant increases in bulimic symptoms observed in controls because such prophylactic effects are rare.

Efficacy Trial 2

Although the above findings were encouraging, in our second evaluation we sought to improve on the first trial by using a larger sample, random assignment to condition, and an active control condition (Stice, Chase, Stormer, & Appel, 2001). We compared our intervention to an active control group to rule out the possibility that expectancies or demand characteristics accounted for the intervention effects. We selected a healthy weight management intervention as our active control group because past trials of this type of psychoeducational program had not produced significant effects (Killen et al., 1993; Smolak, Levine & Schermer, 1998). In the healthy weight intervention, participants were told that body image concerns are based on incomplete information about effective weight control behaviors. The intervention provided information about nutrition and exercise and used behavioral change techniques to help participants design an individualized healthy diet and exercise program.

We randomly assigned 87 high-risk young women (M age = 19) with body image concerns to the Body Project intervention ("dissonance intervention") or healthy weight interventions. Dissonance participants showed significant decreases in thin-ideal internalization, body dissatisfaction, dietary restraint scores, negative affect, and bulimic symptoms from pretest to posttest and pretest to 1-month follow-up. Unexpectedly, healthy weight participants also showed significant decreases in the latter three outcomes. It was reassuring that the reductions in thin-ideal internalization and body dissatisfaction were significantly stronger in the dissonance treatment than in the healthy weight treatment, as this provided some evidence that the former intervention was superior. However, the changes in the other three outcomes did not differ across conditions. Participants assigned to assessment-only control conditions in past prevention trials did not show decreases in these outcomes, which suggests that the healthy weight intervention effects cannot easily be attributed to a measurement artifact or regression to the mean. The fact that most eating disorder prevention programs have not produced reductions in eating pathology suggests that the healthy weight effects cannot be easily attributed to expectancies or demand characteristics. It seemed more likely that we inadvertantly developed an alternate effective prevention program.

Efficacy Trial 3

Because the positive intervention effects for the healthy weight intervention were challenging to interpret, we conducted a third efficacy trial that compared the dissonance intervention to a healthy weight intervention and a waitlist control group (Stice, Trost et al., 2003). We improved upon the past trial by extending the follow-up to 6 months, recruiting a larger sample, and intervening before the period of peak risk for eating pathology onset. We also included a waitlist comparison group to permit a less ambiguous interpretation of the findings. In this trial, 148 high-risk adolescent girls (M age = 17) with body image concerns were randomly assigned to the three conditions. Participants in both interventions reported significantly greater reduction in negative affect and bulimic symptoms at posttest and at follow-up relative to controls, although no significant effects were observed for thin-ideal internalization, body dissatisfaction, or dieting. Relative to healthy weight participants, dissonance participants showed significantly greater reductions in thin-ideal internalization, body dissatisfaction, negative affect, and bulimic symptoms from pretest to posttest and for negative affect from pretest to follow-up.

Large-Scale Efficacy Trial

Next, we initiated a large-scale efficacy trial to further test the efficacy of the dissonance and healthy weight interventions (funded by National Institutes of Health grant MH/DK 61957). This efficacy trial improved upon previous research by incorporating blinded diagnostic interviews, a larger sample, enhanced group leader training, and a 3-year follow-up. In this four-group trial, 481 body-dissatisfied adolescent girls (M age = 17) recruited from several high schools and one university were randomized to the Body Project, the healthy weight intervention, an expressive writing control condition, or an assessment-only control condition. Students with a *DSM-IV* eating disorder were excluded from the trial and provided with a treatment referral for more intensive intervention. Participants are now completing pretest, posttest, 6-month, 12-month, 24-month, and 36-month assessments.

Although this trial is ongoing, we have examined the intervention effects through the 12-month follow-up (Stice, Shaw, Burton, & Wade, 2006). Relative to assessment-only controls, Body Project participants showed significantly greater reductions in thin-ideal internalization, body dissatisfaction, dieting, negative affect, and bulimic symptoms at posttest and 6-month follow-up, and in thin-ideal internalization, dieting, and bulimic symptoms at 12-month follow-up. Body Project participants also showed significantly greater reductions in all five outcomes relative to healthy weight and expressive writing participants at posttest. Relative to expressive writing participants, Body Project participants showed significantly greater reductions in body dissatisfaction, dieting, negative affect, and bulimic symptoms at 6-month follow-up and in dieting at 12-month follow-up. Body Project participants showed significantly greater reductions in negative affect relative to healthy weight participants at both 6- and 12-month follow-up.

Relative to assessment-only controls, healthy weight participants showed significantly greater reductions in thin-ideal internalization, body dissatisfaction, and negative affect at posttest, in thin-ideal internalization, body dissatisfaction, dieting, and bulimic symptoms at 6-month follow-up, and in thin-ideal internalization, dieting, and bulimic symptoms at 12-month follow-up. Healthy weight participants showed significantly greater reductions, relative to expressive-writing controls, in thin-ideal internalization, body dissatisfaction, negative affect, and bulimic symptoms at posttest, in body dissatisfaction and bulimic symptoms at 6-month follow-up, and in thin-ideal internalization at 12-month follow-up. Expressive writing participants did not differ from assessment-only controls for virtually all outcomes. Potentially expanding the public health significance of these interventions, dissonance and healthy weight participants showed significantly lower incidences of binge eating and obesity onset and reduced service utilization through 12-month follow-up. Although we are still in the process of collecting the 36-month follow-up data, preliminary analyses suggest that most of the effects that were significant at 12-month follow-up are still significant at 24-month follow-up and that some additional effects become significant (e.g., for psychosocial functioning).

Another study investigated the mediators hypothesized to account for the effects of the dissonance and healthy weight interventions (Stice, Presnell, Gau, & Shaw, 2007). The dissonance intervention produced significant reductions in outcomes (body dissatisfaction, dieting, negative affect, bulimic symptoms) and in the mediator (thin-ideal internalization); change in the mediator predicted change in outcomes and usually occurred before change in outcomes; and intervention effects became significantly weaker when change in the mediator was controlled for, providing support for the hypothesized mediators. The healthy weight intervention produced significant reductions in outcomes (body dissatisfaction, negative affect, bulimic symptoms) and increases in the mediators (healthy eating and physical activity), and changes in the mediators occurred before changes in outcomes. However, change in the mediator only predicted change in outcomes for half of the effects, although the intervention effects generally did become significantly weaker when change in the mediator was controlled for. These results provide somewhat weaker support for the hypothesized mediators for the healthy weight intervention.

Large-Scale Effectiveness Trial

Given the promising data from the four efficacy trials, we initiated an effectiveness trial of the Body Project (funded by National Institutes of Health grant MH 70699). This study, which is one of the first large-scale effectiveness trials of an eating disorder prevention program, was designed to determine whether this program produces positive effects when delivered by school counselors, nurses, and teachers in real-world settings (high schools) under ecologically valid conditions. Our goal is to randomly assign 330 high-risk adolescent girls to the dissonance intervention or to a psychoeducational brochure control condition and follow them over a 2-year period. To date, 182 young women from three high schools (Mage = 16) have been enrolled and randomized to condition. Preliminary results from the first 86 participants who have provided data through 6-month follow-up indicate that relative to control participants, dissonance participants show significantly greater reductions in thin-ideal internalization, body dissatisfaction, dieting, negative affect, and bulimic symptoms from pretreatment to posttreatment. However, only the effects for bulimic symptoms reached significance with this limited sample size at 6-month follow-up. These preliminary results provide evidence that this intervention may produce desirable effects when delivered by "natural" providers in the real world.

Independent Evaluations of the Body Project

To date, four independent labs that have evaluated versions of the dissonance-based Body Project eating disorder prevention program. Becker, Jilka, and Polvere (2002) randomized female college students to a two-session version of the Body Project or a two-session media literacy intervention. Both interventions reduced body dissatisfaction, dieting, and eating disorder symptoms, but the Body Project also resulted in decreased thin-ideal internalization and significantly greater reductions in body dissatisfaction than the media literacy program. In another study, Becker, Smith, and Ciao (2005) randomized female college students to the Body Project, a media literacy intervention, or a waitlist control group. Both interventions produced significantly greater reductions in dieting, body dissatisfaction, and eating disorder symptoms relative to controls, but only the Body Project produced significantly greater reductions in thin-ideal internalization relative to controls. Becker, Smith and Ciao (2005) randomized female college students to the Body Project or a media literacy intervention. Although both interventions showed equivalent reductions in bulimic symptoms at an 8-month follow-up, the Body Project resulted in significantly greater reductions in thin-ideal internalization, body dissatisfaction, and dieting.

Matusek, Wendt, and Wiseman (2004) randomized female college students with body image concerns to a single 2-hour Body Project intervention, a single 2-hour healthy weight-control intervention, or a wait-list control condition. Both interventions resulted in significantly greater reductions in thin-ideal internalization and eating disorder symptoms relative to controls, but there were no significant differences between the two interventions.

Green et al. (2005) randomized female college students to either a one-session high-dissonance version of the Body Project, a one-session low dissonance version of the Body project, or an assessment-only control condition. Participants in the high-dissonance condition reported fewer eating disorder symptoms than participants in the low-dissonance condition at posttest, although no differences were found between participants in either intervention condition relative to controls. Roehrig et al. (2006) randomized female college students with body image concerns to the original version of the Body Project or to a version with only the dissonance-inducing exercises: both interventions produced significant but comparable reductions in body dissatisfaction, dieting, and bulimic symptoms.

A more comprehensive review of the results of these trials can be found on the companion Web site at www.oup.com/us/ttw.

Summary of Prevention Trials

The prevention trials described above have a number of important implications. First, the fact that dissonance interventions produced intervention effects for eating pathology and risk factors for eating pathology in a variety of independent studies suggests that the effects of this type of intervention are replicable. This replication is particularly noteworthy because several labs received no direct training in the intervention delivery. Indeed, Becker (Becker, Jilka, & Polvere, 2002; Becker, Smith, & Ciao, 2005) developed an intervention script for her first two trials based solely on the brief description of the intervention provided in the Stice, Mazotti et al. (2000) article, suggesting that minor variations in the implementation of this intervention have little impact on its effectiveness. It is also striking that the various trials evaluated somewhat different versions of this intervention, but that each version produced positive effects.

Second, it is noteworthy that the Body Project has shown positive effects when delivered to both general (universal) and high-risk (selected) samples and that several studies found that the intervention effects were similar for low- and high-risk subgroups (Becker et al., 2005; Green et al., 2005). These results suggest that this intervention may be appropriate for a variety of populations. Although most of the prevention trials previously reviewed focused on selected samples, certain investigators and clinicians favor universal programs because they more effectively challenge the ecology of eating disorders—the peer groups, family, and sociocultural environment that purportedly contribute to the development and persistence of these disorders (Levine & Smolak, 2006). For instance, a targeted school-based program may backfire if a participant's efforts to resist unhealthy dieting are thwarted by peers engaging in discussions that perpetuate the thin ideal. Others argue for universal prevention because they believe that risk factors are normally distributed in the population and that the largest proportion of cases will emerge from the low-to-moderate, rather from than the high-risk group (Austin, 2001).

Third, it is reassuring that this intervention produced positive effects when delivered by both research-trained staff and existing providers (e.g., health educators). Even more striking is the evidence that this intervention produced positive effects when delivered by undergraduate students (Becker, Ciao, Smith et al., 2005). Thus, it appears that, given appropriate training, this intervention can be effectively delivered by a range of group leaders, an essential criterion for dissemination.

Fourth, the Body Project produced positive effects when participants received compensation for participating in the trial as well as when they did not. These findings imply that the positive effects are not simply due to monetary compensation and that adolescent girls and young women will sign up for the intervention even if they are not compensated.

Fifth, the Body Project produced significantly stronger effects relative to four alternative credible interventions (Becker et al., 2002; Becker, Smith, Bell et al., 2005; Green et al., 2005; Stice et al., 2003; Stice, Shaw, Burton et al., 2006). Although these effects were limited to certain outcome variables and generally did not persist over longer follow-up periods, the results are striking because they represent the most rigorous test of an intervention given that comparison to an alternative intervention controls for demand characteristics, client expectancies, and nonspecific treatment factors. We know of no other previously evaluated eating disorder or obesity prevention program that has produced significantly stronger effects relative to active alternative prevention programs or placebo interventions.

Finally, it is encouraging that the Body Project produced effects for other clinically meaningful outcomes, including mental health care utilization and obesity. If replicated, the finding that this intervention resulted in a threefold decrease in risk for obesity onset relative to assessment-only controls may have highly significant public health implications because virtually no obesity prevention program has reduced risk for future obesity onset (Stice, Shaw, & Marti, 2006). In addition, these findings suggest that a single, brief intervention may produce positive effects for both eating pathology and obesity.

Alternative Eating Disorder Prevention Programs

The summary of a recent meta-analysis of eating disorder prevention programs revealed that only 6 of the 38 eating disorder prevention programs that have been evaluated in controlled trials produced reductions in current or future symptoms that persisted over follow-up, which ranged from 1 to 24 months (Stice & Shaw, 2004). Two of these prevention programs were the Body Project program and the healthy weight program discussed previously in detail. In the section that follows, we describe the other four eating disorder prevention programs that produced intervention effects for eating pathology. Although each of these alternative programs holds promise, the evidence base for these programs is limited.

Neumark-Sztainer, Butler, and Palti (1995) evaluated a 10-hour universal intervention that was offered to all female students in participating schools, which presented information on healthy weight control behaviors, body image, eating disorders, causes of eating disorders, and social pressure resistance skills. The program produced significant improvements in eating disorder symptoms at 1-month follow-up; in dieting and binge eating at 6-month follow-up; and in binge eating at 24-month follow-up relative to assessment-only controls.

Stewart, Carter, Drinkwater, Hainsworth, and Fairburn (2001) evaluated a 5-hour universal program that focused on resisting cultural pressures for thinness, body weight determinants, body acceptance, effects of cognitions on emotions, nature and consequences of eating disorders, self-esteem enhancement, stress management, and healthy weight control behaviors. It produced significant improvements in dieting and eating disorder symptoms at termination and at 6-month follow-up and decreases in body dissatisfaction at termination, relative to assessment-only controls.

Bearman, Stice, and Chase (2003) evaluated a 4-hour targeted cognitive-behavioral intervention designed to promote body satisfaction among high-risk women with body image concerns by replacing negative appearance self-statements with positive statements and by using systematic desensitization to reduce body image anxiety. The program produced significant reductions in body dissatisfaction, negative affect, and bulimic symptoms at termination and at 3-month follow-up, and in body dissatisfaction at 6-month follow-up relative to waitlist controls.

McVey, Lieberman, Voorberg, Wardrope, and Blackmore (2003) evaluated a 10-hour targeted program that promoted critical media use, body acceptance, healthy weight control behaviors, and stress management skills and provided information regarding body mass determinants. It produced significantly greater decreases in body dissatisfaction, dieting, and bulimic symptoms than observed in assessment-only controls at both termination and at 3-month follow-up. However, these effects were not replicated in a second trial (McVey, Lieberman, Voorberg, Wardrope, Blackmore, & Tweed, 2003).

In summary, the dissonance-based Body Project intervention program has decreased eating pathology and risk factors for eating pathology in treated subjects relative to an assessment-only control condition in four trials in our lab. In trials conducted by four independent labs, the Body Project intervention was superior to four alternative interventions in multiple trials, and it produced effects that persisted through 1-year follow-up. This intervention has produced true prophylactic effects, in that it reduced risk for onset of or future increases in bulimic symptoms over follow-up. Evidence also suggests that the Body Project produces effects for other important public health outcomes, including mental health care utilization and risk for obesity onset.

Based on data from these prevention trials, it appears that the dissonance intervention has now received enough empirical support to be categorized as efficacious, setting it apart from other eating disorder prevention programs. According to the American Psychological Association (1995), an intervention has to have produced significantly stronger effects than a waitlist or measurement-only control condition in at least two trials conducted by independent labs and significantly stronger effects than a placebo or alternative treatment to be considered an empirically supported intervention. It is important to note that the healthy weight intervention has also received enough empirical support to be considered an efficacious intervention. It is therefore tempting to consider integrating the dissonance intervention with the healthy weight intervention because such an integrated program may yield larger intervention effects relative to either individual intervention. Part II of this guide describes the four-session version of the Healthy Weight eating disorder prevention program, which may be administered after completion of the Body Project, if group leaders think it would be useful.

Session 1

2

Materials Needed

- Flip chart (or whiteboard) and markers
- Attendance sheet
- Facilitator Fact sheet (see appendix)
- Pictures of models from fashion magazines (group leaders should cut out 10–20 and place in plastic sleeves)
- Letter to Adolescent Girl form
- Self-Affirmation form

Session Outline

- Make introductions
- Present conceptual rationale for intervention, group rules, and expectations
- Provide a definition of the thin ideal
- Discuss costs associated with the thin ideal
- Assign home exercises

Overview

The focus of session 1 is on providing a conceptual rationale and overview of the program, introducing participants to each other, and orienting participants to the rules and expectations of the group. This initial session is largely interactive, with participant-led discussions of the definition and origins of the thin ideal, and costs associated with pursuing the thin ideal. The group leader should stress the importance of attendance and completing the home exercises. The general goal of this session is for participants to begin to critically evaluate the thin ideal and to begin inducing dissonance by having them make public counter-attitudinal statements.

You should read the script that appears in italic font. Instructions appear in nonitalic font. Also, please try to follow the recommended time limits for each section, which will ensure that all of the content is covered.

Introduction (5 minutes)

At the start of the first session, welcome the members of the group and provide a brief description of the program.

Thanks for joining us. All of you decided to take part in these groups because of your body image concerns—an issue very common among girls and women.

This class is based on studies that found when women talk about the "thin ideal" and how to challenge pressures to be thin, it makes them feel better about their bodies. It is based on the idea that understanding the cultural pressures that influence women's body images and learning how to respond to these pressures improves body satisfaction. Research has shown that this is one of the best classes for improving body satisfaction, and it also lowers the rates of obesity, eating problems, and depression.

You should then introduce yourself to the group. Introductions include name, professional status, and personal information (e.g., something interesting or unique about yourself). Ask the coleader (if part of the group) and group members to introduce themselves. This is an opportunity for you to break the ice and help participants feel comfortable discussing personal thoughts and experiences.

Let's start by getting to know each other better. Can each of you tell us your name, your year in school, and something unique or interesting about you?

Spend a few moments with each participant to elicit specific information and show interest (e.g., "How long have you been horseback riding?" "What kind of paintings do you do?"). Taking the time to have participants get to know one another helps facilitate group cohesion.

Voluntary Commitment and Overview (2 minutes)

After the introductions have been completed, ask the group members if they are willing to voluntarily commit to participating in the class.

The main idea in this class is that discussing the social pressures behind body dissatisfaction and how to respond to them will improve your body satisfaction. Experience suggests that people get the most out of these groups if they attend all four meetings, participate verbally, and complete all of the between-meeting exercises. Are you willing to do this?

Go around the room and have each participant say they are willing to actively participate (a simple "yes" from each participant will suffice). It is important to solicit verbal commitment to engage in the sessions and activities because it increases the level of investment in the group and may help achieve a higher level of dissonance. Once group members express their commitment to the class, provide them with a verbal outline of the program (see table 2.1).

Table 2.1 Program Outline

1. *Define* the thin-ideal and explore its origin.
2. Examine the *costs* of pursuing this ideal.
3. Explore ways to *resist* pressures to be thin.
4. Discuss how to *challenge* our personal body-related concerns.
5. Learn new ways to *talk more positively* about our bodies, and
6. Talk about how we can best respond to *future* pressures to be thin.

Confidentiality

It is important to discuss the issue of confidentiality with the group because personal details of some of the group members' lives may be revealed throughout the course of the program. Additionally, when this intervention is conducted in settings such as high schools or sororities, there may be participants in the group who know each other or may come into contact outside of the group. It is critical that participants, particularly adolescents, feel confident that anything they share will not be repeated to anyone outside of the group in order to facilitate their discussion of personal experiences that may be embarrassing or sensitive.

While we are going through the different parts of this class, some of us will probably reveal some personal details about our lives. This can be difficult when we are not sure if we can trust that others won't repeat what we've said. So we ask that everything said in our group remains completely confidential. Can everyone agree to this?

Attendance

Stress the importance of attending all classes.

It is also important that everyone attends all four sessions of this group. If for some reason you need to miss a session, please let me (or the coleader) know as soon as possible. We will need to schedule a make-up session with you before the next regular group session so you will be caught up with everyone else.

You should call or email participants the day before each session to remind them of the session and to remind them to bring any assignments that are due. If a participant must miss a session, schedule a brief (15 minute) individual make-up session to discuss key points from the session so that the participant will be caught up for the next session. Ask them to complete the home exercises before the next session. These make-up sessions are an important key to the success of this intervention; they send a clear message to the participants that it is important for them to attend each session. If it is known at the outset that a participant will not be able to attend all scheduled sessions (e.g., due to vacation or a previously scheduled event) or must leave a session early, set up an individual makeup session ahead of time. If the participant anticipates

Attendance Sheet

Record names of participants and check if they attend each session. This will assist you in knowing who to contact for an individual make-up session, if they miss a session.

Names of participants in the group:	Session 1	Session 2	Session 3	Session 4
1. _____	•	•	•	•
2. _____	•	•	•	•
3. _____	•	•	•	•
4. _____	•	•	•	•
5. _____	•	•	•	•
6. _____	•	•	•	•
7. _____	•	•	•	•
8. _____	•	•	•	•
9. _____	•	•	•	•
10. _____	•	•	•	•
11. _____	•	•	•	•
12. _____	•	•	•	•

missing more than one session at the outset, they should be scheduled for another group if possible because the group context theoretically helps facilitate attitudinal change. We have included an attendance sheet because it helps group leaders know who has missed particular sessions.

Definition and Origin of the Thin Ideal (15 minutes)

Spread out pictures from magazines showing a variety of models on the table (there should be at least enough pictures for each participant to select one). Direct the group members to choose one picture that appeals to them in some way. Do not tell participants the purpose of this exercise—just ask them to pick one that is appealing to them. After they have chosen, ask each group member to tell you what they notice about the picture and what it says about society's view of women.

See the Facilitator Fact sheet in the appendix for assorted statistics and findings that will help you facilitate the following discussion points. The fact sheet lists many points of interest that will make for a more lively discussion.

Pose questions to the group and promote participation and collaboration on their responses. Promoting discussion is key—let participants do the talking, rather than you and the coleader. If participants sense that group leaders are trying to coax certain responses from them, this may decrease any dissonance associated with their counter-attitudinal statements. In general, experience indicates that taking a stance of interested curiosity seems to work best.

What are we told that the "perfect woman" looks like?

Possible answers include: thin and attractive, a perfect body, toned, large-breasted, tall, look like a super-model.

Focus the discussion on the thin and unrealistic parts of the thin ideal, though it is fine to note other aspects, such as a clear complexion and white teeth. Note incompatible features, such as ultraslenderness coupled with large breasts. Make an effort to be culturally sensitive, and acknowledge that the cultural ideal differs for different ethnic groups. Participants may bring this up as a topic of conversation, in which case you should use this opportunity to explore how both the dominant culture and subcultures influence our perceptions of beauty ideals.

Write down each of the qualities on a whiteboard or flipchart. Explain to the group that these qualities represent the thin ideal, which will be the main focus of ensuing discussions. This exercise helps ensure that participants have a shared understanding and visual representation of the thin ideal.

Has this thin ideal always been the ideal for feminine attractiveness? Has there ever been a time in history when the "perfect woman" looked different?

Solicit examples of different beauty standards over time (e.g., Marilyn Monroe, women of the Renaissance period, Twiggy, supermodels of today).

Where did this ideal come from? What are the origins of the thin ideal in our current society?

Possible answers include media, the fashion industry, and the diet/weight loss industry. Posing this question helps elicit responses that indicate that this ideal is not internally generated, but rather it is promoted by industries that have a vested interest in the way in which we perceive our bodies.

How is the thin ideal promoted to us?

Possible answers include television shows, magazines, and music videos. This may also include influences in more immediate subcultures, such as peers and family members.

How do thin-ideal messages from your family, friends, and dating partners affect how you feel emotionally?

Discuss this with each group member and relate it to her personal experiences in these areas and the impact on her feelings and self-worth. Participants may share emotional or distressing experiences that they have encountered. Respond empathically and allow group members to interact with one another, while ensuring that the discussion remains on track.

How do thin-ideal messages from the media impact the way you feel about your body? What are your thoughts and feelings about your own body when you look at a magazine picture of the thin ideal?

Possible answers include feeling inadequate because I do not look like a model, dislike of my own body, or makes me depressed.

What does our culture tell us will happen if we are able to look like the thin ideal?

Possible answers include we will be accepted, loved, happy, successful, and wealthy.

Do you really think these good things happen if you get thinner?

Discuss the fact that becoming thinner will likely have little impact on their lives in terms of these perceived benefits.

Be sure to differentiate the thin ideal from the healthy ideal if group members say people are healthier if they conform to the thin ideal. Be careful not to convey that trying to be healthy is bad—briefly make a distinction between the healthy ideal and the thin ideal (avoiding obesity and resulting health consequences versus striving for an unrealistic look by whatever means necessary). However, do not describe (or allow participants to discuss) the benefits of thinness in general or give the impression that the thin ideal is close to the healthy ideal (i.e., it is possible to be well within the healthy weight range, but not meet the cultural standards for the ultrathin ideal). It is vital for group leaders to make sure that any discussions of the benefits of thinness are redirected back to a discussion of the costs of pursuing the thin ideal. A sample redirection statement is, "Although there are clearly medical problems associated with obesity, the goal of the present session is to discuss the costs of pursuing the ultraslender ideal promoted by our culture."

Costs Associated with Pursuing the Thin Ideal (20 minutes)

With participation from the group, discuss the costs involved with the thin ideal.

For the individual person, what are the costs of trying to look like the thin ideal?

Possible answers include decreased self-worth, financial expense, physical and mental exhaustion, and adverse physical effects due to extreme dieting or exercise. You may have to ask group members to take a few moments to think about these questions. Pause and wait for group members to respond, rather than suggesting responses.

How does the thin ideal negatively affect people's health?

Possible answers include: encourages unhealthy weight management techniques, can cause depression and anxiety.

What are the costs for society?

Possible answers include increased mental health care costs and promotes a culture of discontent.

Who benefits from the thin ideal?

Possible answers include media, the fashion industry, and the diet/weight loss industry.

Are you one of the people who benefit from the thin ideal? For example, are you a media executive, a supermodel, the founder of a diet program?

Given all these costs, does it make sense to try to look like the thin ideal?

Make sure that *each participant* makes a public statement against the thin ideal at this stage (and anywhere else possible). It is important, however, not to engage in a battle of wills with participants. In such cases, it is generally best to rely on other group members to challenge each other.

Home Exercises (3 minutes)

Assign the following home exercises and ask a member of the group to paraphrase the assignments back to you to make sure that they understand each home exercise. When assigning home exercises, it is important to provide verbal instructions on how to use each form.

- Have each group member use the Letter to Adolescent Girl form in the workbook to write a letter to a teenage girl who is struggling with her body image, focusing on the costs associated with trying to look like the thin ideal. Group members may work with a family member or friend to generate ideas.

- Have each group member fill-out the Self-Affirmation form in the workbook. Introduce the form using the following dialogue:

We would like to ask you to stand in front of a mirror and look at yourself and write down all your positive qualities. This includes physical, emotional, intellectual, and social qualities. For instance, you may like the shape of your arms, the strength of your legs, your hair, the sound of your laugh, or the fact that you are a good friend. We know it can be hard, but please make sure to

Letter to Adolescent Girl

Please write a letter to an adolescent girl who is struggling with body image concerns about the costs associated with pursuing the thin ideal. Think of as many costs as you can. Feel free to work with a friend or family member in generating ideas or use any of the ones we discussed in the group. Please bring this letter to our next meeting so we can discuss your responses and feelings about this assignment.

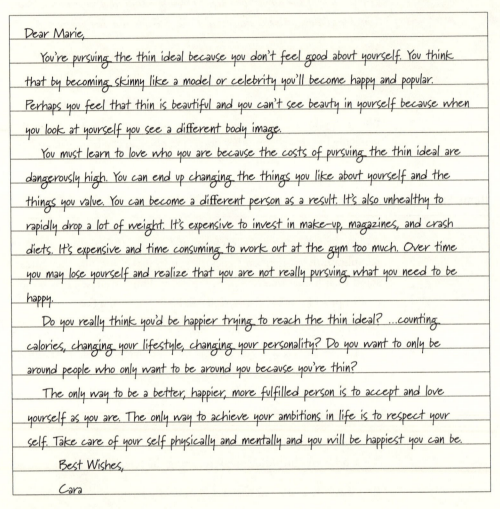

Dear Marie,

You're pursuing the thin ideal because you don't feel good about yourself. You think that by becoming skinny like a model or celebrity you'll become happy and popular. Perhaps you feel that thin is beautiful and you can't see beauty in yourself because when you look at yourself you see a different body image.

You must learn to love who you are because the costs of pursuing the thin ideal are dangerously high. You can end up changing the things you like about yourself and the things you value. You can become a different person as a result. It's also unhealthy to rapidly drop a lot of weight. It's expensive to invest in make-up, magazines, and crash diets. It's expensive and time consuming to work out at the gym too much. Over time you may lose yourself and realize that you are not really pursuing what you need to be happy.

Do you really think you'd be happier trying to reach the thin ideal? ...counting calories, changing your lifestyle, changing your personality? Do you want to only be around people who only want to be around you because you're thin?

The only way to be a better, happier, more fulfilled person is to accept and love yourself as you are. The only way to achieve your ambitions in life is to respect your self. Take care of your self physically and mentally and you will be happiest you can be.

Best Wishes,

Cara

Figure 2.1

Example of Completed Letter to Adolescent Girl

Self-Affirmation Exercise

Please stand in front of a mirror and look at yourself and write down all your positive qualities. This includes physical, emotional, intellectual, and social qualities. For instance, you may like the shape of your arms, the strength of your legs, your long dark hair, the sound of your laugh, or the fact that you are a good friend. Please make sure to include at least some physical attributes on your list.

- My long legs
- My big eyes
- My hair color
- My mellow attitude
- My artistic skills
- My ability to dance silly
- My hands and fingers
- My cheeks
- My feet
- My outlook on life
- My logic
- My ability to make people laugh
- My quirkiness

- My strong opinions
- How I treat the environment
- My knees
- My arm span
- My devotion to journaling
- My curvy hips
- My teeth
- My ability to see beauty around me
- My generosity
- My curiosity
- My taste in fashion
- How supportive I am of my family

Figure 2.2

Example of Completed Self-Affirmation Exercise Form

include at least some physical attributes on your list. It may be difficult at first and may seem silly, but we really want you to do this because it is important to recognize each of these areas about yourself. Past participants have found this exercise to be very helpful and empowering. So give it a shot, and please bring your list of positive qualities to group next week.

Discuss any questions regarding the home exercises and thank group members for their participation.

Session 2

3

Materials Needed

- Verbal Challenge form
- Top-10 List form

Session Outline

- Review home exercises from previous session
- Engage in role-playing exercises
- Assign home exercises

Overview

Before session 2, we strongly recommend that you e-mail or call each group member and remind them to complete the homework exercises and bring their completed forms to the session. The focus of session 2 is on reviewing the topics discussed in the previous session and discusing reactions to the two homework assignments. Then this session moves to role plays to elicit verbal statements against the thin ideal.

In this session, we will talk more about the costs of pursuing the thin ideal and explore ways that we can resist pressures to be thin.

Letter Review (15 minutes)

Begin the session by soliciting comments from the group regarding their thoughts about the letter-writing exercise. Some questions to ask are:

Did you find this exercise difficult?

What were your feelings as you wrote the letter?

Who is willing to read a part of the letter they wrote?

Have *each participant* read aloud several of the costs she identified in her letter. A key idea is that by verbalizing ways in which the thin ideal is detrimental on many different levels, participants will increase cognitive dissonance regarding their own subscription to the thin ideal. Encourage group discussion, and engage participants in personalizing these costs to their own lives.

Where there any other costs to pursuing the thin-ideal that you thought of that have not been mentioned?

Self-Affirmation Exercise Review (10 minutes)

Continue the session by soliciting comments from the group regarding their thoughts about and experiences with the self-affirmation exercise. Some questions to ask are:

How did you feel when you did this exercise?

Was it challenging? How so?

Why do we have this culture of shame/humbleness about ourselves? (e.g., media and industry perpetuating thin-ideal)

What are two aspects of yourself that you are satisfied with, including one physical feature?

Have *each participant* share two of the qualities she listed. Discourage "qualified" statements (e.g., "I guess my stomach is not too horrible"). If you get qualified statements, accept them and ask the participant for an additional statement that is completely positive (e.g., "Okay, can you give me one more statement that is completely positive?"). Participants often comment that this exercise is difficult because they feel conceited or feel as though they are bragging, and they may express concern that others will view them negatively for stating what they like about themselves. It is important to reiterate that this group is meant to be a safe place for them to discuss these topics. If participants remain reluctant to share their positive qualities, this can facilitate a discussion of why they find it difficult to talk about what they like about themselves, yet they readily identify flaws. You may have participants contrast the number of times they find fault with their bodies with how many positive statements they make about themselves, and discuss how our culture supports this type of negative self-talk.

In the end, did you feel the exercise was useful? . . . Hopefully, you recognize the positive things about yourselves and will remember them, particularly as the pressure of the thin ideal surrounds you. Given that these are potent pressures, let's discuss ways to resist them.

Role Plays to Discourage Pursuit of the Thin Ideal (20 minutes)

Group leaders should take the role of either a severe dieter or an eating-disordered individual as *each participant* responds. Let each participant spend approximately 2 minutes attempting to dissuade you from pursuing the thin ideal. Parrot, or echo, any pro–thin-ideal comments previously made by participants while you are playing the thin-ideal role. Doing so will force participants to develop counter arguments against their own pro–thin-ideal statements. Focus on the unrealistic benefits of the thin ideal ("I'll be happy all the time if I'm thin," "Everyone will like me," "I'll have the perfect partner," "All my problems will be solved"). Make sure each participant tries to talk you out of pursuing the thin ideal.

Now I would like to do some role plays. I will play a person who is obsessed with the thin ideal and your job will be to convince me that I shouldn't be. Feel free to use any of the information brought up in our earlier discussions.

Select group members to participate, making sure *each participant* has a turn. If you have time, ask each participant to engage in two role plays.

Sample statements for leaders include:

■ *Swimsuit season is just around the corner, and so I think I will start skipping breakfasts to take off some extra weight.*

■ *I am sure that people will accept me and love me if I only lose a little more weight.*

■ *I just saw an ad for this new weight loss pill. I'm going to order it right away. I can finally be as thin as I want.*

■ *I can't meet you for dinner tonight because I have to go spend a few hours at the gym. I only went for two hours yesterday.*

■ *I feel a little dizzy lately, which may be from these diet pills I'm on, but I don't care because I've already lost 10 pounds.*

■ *Most people have weak will power and give in to hunger. I'll show people how much self-control I have by not eating anything but grapefruit.*

■ *To be the best runner, I have to get down to my lightest weight. I am only doing this for my health; this will help me avoid injuries.*

■ *I have to be thin or my life is ruined.*

■ *Anyone could have the body of a supermodel if they really wanted it.*

■ *No guy is ever going to ask me to the prom unless I drop some of this weight.*

You should generate additional statements as needed, and you may tailor the statements to be appropriate for their group members.

Role Play Debriefing

Ask the group members how it felt to do the role plays. Let them reflect on how it felt to argue against someone who is fixated on pursuing the thin ideal.

Do you think it might be beneficial for you to challenge people when they make thin-ideal statements?

Promote discussion of why it is helpful to speak out against pressure to conform to the thin ideal. Let participants come up with the arguments.

Home Exercises (3 minutes)

Verbal Challenges Home Exercise

When assigning home exercises, it is important to provide verbal instructions on how to use each form.

■ Ask group members to first come up with examples from their real lives of pressures to be thin using the Verbal Challenge form in the workbook and then generate verbal challenges to these thin ideal comments. Introduce the form using the following dialogue.

Here are some examples of thin-ideal statements:

1. A boyfriend might say that he thinks the ideal dress size is a 2.

2. Your mom might comment on how another mom has really let herself go because she gained some weight.

3. A friend could say that she wished she looked like a particular super-model when looking at a fashion magazine.

How could you respond to these comments to show that you disagree with the thin ideal and think these sorts of comment are unhealthy?

In this first home exercise, please come up with at least three examples from your life and how you could have responded verbally to challenges. These examples probably won't be how you actually responded to the pressure. Instead, they should be how you might respond now based on what you know about the thin ideal.

■ Instruct group members to generate a verbal challenge to each pressure they generated, just as they did in the role plays during this session.

Top 10 List Home Exercise

■   Ask group members to generate a list of things girls/women can do to resist the thin ideal and write them down on the Top-10 List form in the workbook. Introduce the form using the following dialogue.

The second exercise is to come up with a top-10 list of things girls/women can do to resist the thin ideal. What can you avoid, say, do, or learn to battle this unhealthy beauty ideal? Please write your top-10 list down and bring it to the next group.

Encourage participants to be creative with this exercise. Elicit one or two examples, such as:

1. Write letter to fashion magazine editor saying they should include a variety of body sizes in the magazine

2. Write a letter to a company indicating that you are boycotting their product because they promote the thin ideal in their ads

3. Stop subscribing to a fashion magazine

4. Stop wearing in vogue clothing that is meant to show slenderness (e.g., tight pants)

Ask one participant to paraphrase the instructions for each exercise to ensure that the group understands the assignments.

Verbal Challange

Please provide examples from your real life concerning pressures to be thin that you have encountered and then write down verbal challenges, like we did in the role-plays.

Here are some examples of thin-ideal statements:

1. A boyfriend might say that he thinks the ideal dress size is a 2.

2. Your mom might comment on how another mom has really let herself go because she gained some weight.

3. A friend could say that she wished she looked like a particular supermodel when looking over a fashion magazine.

Please write down how you could respond to the thin-ideal comments that you generated to indicate that you do not agree with the thin-ideal and think these sorts of comments are unhealthy.

Please come up with at least three such examples from your life and how you could respond to these thin-ideal comments. These responses probably won't be how you actually responded to the pressure. Instead, they should be how you might respond *now* based on what you know about the thin-ideal.

1) *Situation:* A friend says that she thinks women's thighs shouldn't touch.

Verbal Response: Some people have bodies where it's natural for their thighs not to touch, but most women's thighs do touch naturally. Women's thighs are supposed to have muscle and fat. Besides, isn't that a silly thing to be worrying about anyway?

2) *Situation:* A coach tells you that you're starting to get too fat for the team.

Verbal Response: Teens go through many growth stages in life. I'm still able to play just fine, so it really shouldn't matter what I weigh or how much fat is on my body.

3) *Situation:* A friend says that she is only going to drink water for the next couple days in order to lose weight.

Verbal Response: While water is good for you, it is definitely not healthy to only drink water. Your body needs the vitamins and nutrients in the food you eat. You're probably going to feel tired, sick, and unhealthy. Why would you put yourself through that just to lose a couple pounds that you'll probably gain back anyway?

Figure 3.1

Example of Completed Verbal Challenge Form

Top-10 List

Please generate a top-10 list of things girls/women can do to resist the thin-ideal. What can you avoid, say, do, or learn to battle this beauty ideal? Please write your top-10 list down and bring it to the next group.

1) Talk less about body image concerns around friends and family

2) Read less fashion and beauty magazines with skinny models

3) Advocate for healthy eating habits

4) Don't struggle to fit in clothes that only extremely thin people fit into

5) Exercise, build muscle, and stay energetic

6) Try to persuade friends or family that have body image concerns that they should accept their bodies

7) Ask teachers to talk more about resisting the thin-ideal in classes

8) Focus more on work and school, not on TV and magazine models

9) Find out the height and weight ratio of a healthy body

10) Learn more about how to maintain a good diet and healthy lifestyle

Figure 3.2

Example of Completed Top-10 List

Session 3

4

Materials Needed

- Behavioral Challenge form
- Body Activism form

Session Outline

- Review home exercises from previous session
- Engage in role-playing exercises
- Have students share the reasons they were interested in joining the group
- Introduce the Behavioral Exercise
- Introduce concept of "body activism"
- Assign home exercises

Overview

The focus of session 3 is on continuing discussion of how to resist the thin ideal, how to challenge personal body-related concerns, and how to respond to future pressures to be thin. Role plays are again used so that participants can practice making statements that counter the thin ideal.

Verbal Challenge Exercise Review (10 minutes)

Begin the session by asking each group member to share one example from her life of pressures to be thin and the response that the person generated to challenge these thin ideal statements. Solicit one example from *each participant.* If they cannot come up with any examples, encourage them to think of a time when they felt pressure from *themselves* to be thin (e.g., after looking in the mirror or comparing themselves to a thin friend and thinking, "I really should lose weight") and what they could have said to themselves to challenge the thin-ideal thought. Help them understand that pressure can often be subtle and can come in different forms.

Quick Comebacks to Thin-Ideal Statements (10 minutes)

At this stage of the session, you will engage in another role-playing exercise with the group. The goal is to help participants be ready to respond quickly and effectively to pressures to be thin.

Role play using counter thin-ideal statements to resist pressure from peers. Ask *each participant* to generate two counter thin-ideal statements in response to statements that you or your coleader generate. Be sure to ask whether participants ever hear statements like this because it is clinically important to remind them that such harsh statements are freqently uttered. Participants can even generate statements that they have heard others say and use those as examples. Sample statements for leaders include:

- *Look at that fatso over there!*
- *Lindsay has really gained weight over the holidays.*
- *I am thinking of going on a diet, do you want to join me?*
- *Don't you think that girl is a cow?*
- *I would never be friends with someone that heavy.*
- *My brother says I look too fat, what do you think?*
- *Don't you think Jennifer Lopez (or other current media figure) is a little too heavy?*
- *If I don't lose some weight, I may be dropped from the diving team.*
- *I hate my body so much—I wish I could just wake up in a different one.*

- *You know if you just stopped eating cheese, you would lose enough weight to look attractive.*

- *Only skinny girls get asked out by boys.*

- *She really doesn't have the body to be wearing that outfit.*

Role Play Debriefing (15 minutes)

Solicit comments from the group regarding their thoughts about the role-play exercise. How did it make them feel? Encourage group discussion. Participants may bring up that this type of response would be difficult to generate in real life. This can lead into a discussion of some of the challenges to resisting such pressures, which can help group members explore realistic ways in which they might be able to apply these strategies to situations in their own lives.

What things make it hard to resist the thin ideal, and how can we deal with them?

Reasons for Signing up for This Class (10 minutes)

At this point in the class, it is helpful to get group members to share the reasons they were interested in joining the group.

Is anyone willing to share why they signed up for this group? For example, many girls have signed up because of a negative comment somebody made to them, or because of concerns about the shape of their body.

Have participants discuss as much as they are comfortable sharing. The purpose is to allow participants to share specific body image concerns and have the group challenge the thoughts and feelings that participants have about specific body parts. Although group members usually challenge the negative body image thoughts vocalized by each participant, the facilitator should model this behavior for the group if they do not do this automatically. If group members seem reluctant to discuss, the group leaders should acknowledge their own body image concerns that they may have struggled with when they were younger.

Listening to you all, it sounds like it would be helpful to some of you to challenge some of your fears and concerns related to your body image.

Ask group members to talk about the particular things that make each of them feel uncomfortable about their body—for example, wearing certain clothes, going to specific places like a pool or dance club. Often, participants report that they avoid certain activities, places, people, or movements or engage in rituals to hide their perceived physical flaws due to body image concerns. There are usually negative self-statements or predictions that go along with these avoidance practices. The goal of the behavioral challenge is to encourage participants to recognize these self-defeating behaviors and to expose them to their feared situations in order to provide corrective feedback (e.g., in fact people do not point and stare at their bodies when they go to the pool in a swimsuit).

Ask group members if they are willing to do an experiment to help them feel better about their bodies.

We would like to challenge you to do something that you currently do not do because of body image concerns to increase your confidence—for example, wear shorts to school, go to the pool in a swimsuit, or exercise in public. Can you promise to do this at least once in the next week? We would like each of you to do this challenge and then let us know during the next session how it went. Please take a moment to think of something you would like to do but haven't done yet. Each of you should have a plan before we finish today.

Note that the purpose of this exercise is not to simply have participants do something they would not normally do (e.g., wear a tight shirt because it just isn't their style preference), but to do something they would otherwise do *if they did not have body image concerns* (e.g., would *like* to wear a tight shirt but do not because they think it makes their stomach look too fat). It is critical that participants understand this distinction when deciding on a behavioral challenge.

Have *each participant* come up with a behavioral challenge and agree upon what that will be. You should help participants select challenges that are appropriate and that they will be able to do in the next week (e.g., do not select wearing a swimsuit to the pool if it is currently too cold to go to a pool). Also make sure that the participants do not decide to do something that is less healthy, such as overeating some unhealthy food that they usually avoid (e.g., fast food) or cutting out healthy exercise.

Group members can write down their goals on the Behavioral Challenge form in the workbook.

Ask one participant to paraphrase the instructions for the Behavioral Challenge home exercise to ensure that the group understands the directions.

How do you think doing this exercise might help you feel better about your body?

This exercise provides evidence that the fears we have about our bodies are unfounded—people do not stare at our "huge thighs" or "flabby stomach" as we sometimes expect. It also highlights the ways in which participants engage in mind reading and make incorrect inferences about what others may be thinking. For example, because they feel insecure about their appearance, they think, "Everyone who sees me notices how flabby my arms are and are repulsed by them." Facilitators should acknowledge that engaging in these behavioral challenges may take some courage and should make sure that participants understand the rationale behind doing them. Additionally, it is important that participants choose behavioral exercises that are moderately challenging for them, but that they are willing to do. If a participant expresses significant hesitation about doing this exercise, encourage them to consider variations that still tap into their body image concerns but that may be easier to accomplish. For example, if wearing shorts to school is too difficult, participants may be willing to attempt wearing shorts to a shopping mall on the weekend where there may be fewer people they know.

Top-10 List Debriefing (10 minutes)

Review the second homework assignment from session 2. Ask group members to share a few items from their Top-10 List of ways to resist the thin ideal. What can they avoid, say, do, or learn to fight this social pressure? This might be referred to as "body activism."

The second exercise from last session asked you to list 10 things that girls and women could do to resist the thin-ideal—what you can avoid, say, do, or learn to combat this social pressure. This might be referred to as "body activism." Can each of you discuss one or two of the ideas you generated?

Are there specific barriers to actually doing these activities?

How can you overcome these barriers?

We would like each of you to do at least one act of body activism and then let us know how it went. Would you all be willing to do that?

Please choose one behavior from your list to do during the next week. Can each of you tell us what you are planning on doing?

You may want to write your body activism goal on this sheet to remind yourself of it.

Have *each participant* choose one behavior from her Top-10 List to do during the next week. Group members can write down their goals on the Body Activism form in the workbook.

Ask one participant to paraphrase the instructions for the Body Activism home exercise to ensure that the group understands the directions.

Home Exercises

- Ask group members to complete the Behavioral Challenge form.
- Instruct group members to engage in one act of body activism before the next session

Behavioral Challenge

We would like to challenge each of you to do something that you currently do not do because of body image concerns to increase your confidence. For example, wearing shorts to school, going to the pool in a swimsuit, exercising in public. Please do this at least once in the next week. We would like each of you to do this behavioral challenge and then let us know during the next session how it turned out. Please take a moment to think of something you would like to do but haven't done yet. You may wish to write your behavioral goal down on this page to remind yourself of it.

I am going to exercise in front of others (at the gym) for the first time.

Figure 4.1
Example of Completed Behavioral Challenge Form

5

Materials Needed

- Fat Talk List

- Self-Affirmation Exercise form

- Letter to Adolescent Girl form

Session Outline

- Review home exercises from previous session

- Discuss ways to challenge "fat talk"

- Discuss pressures to be thin that group members may experience in the future

- Introduce the concept of positive body talk

- Assign home exercises

Overview

Session 4 focuses on discussing participants' experiences with the behavioral challenge and body activism exercises and talking about how the things we say about our bodies may promote the thin ideal. The activities of this final session include having participants come up with more positive, alternative ways of talking about their bodies and encouraging participants to continue to challenge their body image issues in the future.

Behavioral Exercise Review (10 minutes)

Begin the final session by soliciting comments from the group regarding their thoughts about the behavioral challenge exercise. Some questions to ask are:

Last week we asked you to do something that you do not normally do because of concerns about your body. How did that go?

What did you notice? How did others react to you? Was it what you expected?

What were your thoughts and feelings as you did this?

Did you find this exercise useful? What did you learn?

Try to solicit the idea that nothing catastrophic happened when they did something they had avoided because of body image concerns. Discuss how this exercise influenced their thoughts and feelings about their bodies. Often, participants find that they feel less anxious, frustrated, or shameful about their appearance.

Have *each participant* discuss her experiences. If they did not do the exercise, ask about the barriers to doing it. How can they overcome them? Is there something they can do that might be easier to try out first? Encourage participants to continue to challenge their body-related concerns. Acknowledge that overcoming negative body image takes time and involves ongoing efforts to challenge thoughts and behaviors. Point out that this activity was just one of many ways in which they can challenge some of their body-related concerns, and encourage participants to consider other activities they can do in the future. Although it may seem unnatural at first, getting into the habit of actively confronting their body image concerns can help them change how they feel about their bodies.

I hope you will continue to challenge yourselves and your body image concerns in the future in a similar way.

Praise participants for having the courage to try something new.

Body Activism Exercise Review (10 minutes)

Continue the session by soliciting comments from the participants regarding their thoughts about the body activism exercise. Some questions to ask are:

Last time we also asked you to do one act of body activism. How did that go?

Did you find this exercise difficult?

What were your thoughts and feelings as you did this?

How do you think this type of exercise could make a difference?

Try to let participants talk themselves into doing more of these types of body activism. Have *each participant* discuss her experiences. Encourage participants to explore ways in which they can apply these activities on a regular basis. How might it be beneficial to them and to others?

Challenging Fat Talk (10 minutes)

We've spent a lot of time discussing obvious pressures to be thin that we encounter on a regular basis from the media, friends, and family members. However, we often do not notice some of the more subtle ways the thin ideal is maintained. Can you think of some ways you (or others) might be promoting the thin ideal without even knowing it?

Possible answers include complimenting others on weight loss, joining in when friends complain about their bodies, debating the merits of fad diets, and gossiping about celebrities who are overweight.

Ask group members to open their workbooks to the Fat Talk List, a list of common things we or others often say regarding the thin ideal. **Important note:** Please do *not* have students read any of the Fat Talk statements out loud!

Fat Talk List

1. I'm so fat.

2. I need to lose ten pounds.

3. Do I look fat in this?

4. You think you're fat? Look at me!

5. Gee, you look great. Have you lost weight?

6. I can't eat that—it will make me fat.

7. I'm way too fat to be eating this.

8. I'm too fat to get into a bathing suit.

9. She's too fat to be wearing those pants.

10. She's a little bit too heavy to be dating that guy.

11. You're so thin, how do you do it?

12. Can you believe how much she's let herself go?

13. I've really been doing well on this diet, you should try it.

14. You'd be so pretty if you lost weight.

15. Wow, look at the big butt on that girl!

After students have reviewed the list, engage in a group discussion about the statements. Some questions to ask are:

How do these statements keep the thin-ideal going?

What can you say to stop this sort of talk? Or, how can you change the subject?

How do you think changing the way you talk about your body might impact how you feel about your body and how others respond to you?

Many participants are aware of how negative comments can impact body image, but they have not considered that even seemingly positive statements can reinforce the thin ideal. Try to help participants become more aware of the ways in which they can begin to promote more healthy attitudes about their bodies. Discuss how they may alter their language to be more positive or neutral.

Future Pressures to Be Thin (10 minutes)

At this point in the session, engage the group in a discussion about pressures to be thin that they may face in the future.

We have spent a lot of time discussing past and current experiences regarding pressure to be thin. However, it is important to be prepared to deal with upcoming challenges as well. What are some future pressures to be thin that might come up in your lives?

Possible answers include fitting into a prom dress, senior pictures, summer vacation, "freshman fifteen" (the common belief that students typically gain 15 pounds in their first year of college), pregnancy, and getting older/slower metabolism.

How do you plan on responding to these pressures? It may seem strange to be talking about this now, but it is often easier to come up with responses ahead of time so you are prepared to deal with these pressures when they happen.

Have each participant provide an example of how they will respond to future pressure. If participants have difficulty generating examples, have them think of someone slightly older than they are (e.g., an older sister, friend, or parent) and think about the pressures they have encountered. Although not all situations can be anticipated, many can be identified ahead of time. Are there particular people, situations, or things that trigger these pressures? Encourage participants to visualize themselves applying the strategies they have learned in this group in the anticipated situations and practice responding to them aloud.

Self-Affirmation Exercise (5 minutes)

As the end of the session nears, encourage group members to continue to challenge some of their body-related concerns. Explain to the group that part of doing this is to talk about their bodies in a positive, rather than a negative way. Provide the following ideas to help get them started:

1. Choose one friend or family member and discuss one thing you like about yourselves.

2. Keep a journal of all the good things your body allows you to do (e.g., sleep well and wake up rested, play tennis, play a musical instrument, dance).

3. Pick one friend to make a pact with to avoid negative body talk. When you catch your friend talking negatively about her body, remind her of the pact.

4. Make a pledge to end complaints about your body, such as "I'm so flat chested" or "I hate my legs." When you catch yourself doing this, make a correction by saying something positive about that body part, such as, "I'm so glad my legs got me through soccer practice today."

5. The next time someone gives you a compliment, rather than objecting ("No, I'm so fat"), practice taking a deep breath and saying "Thank you."

Does anyone have any other ideas of ways you can talk more positively about your body?

We would like to ask you to choose one of these activities and do it sometime during the next week and let us know how it goes via e-mail. Consider this an "exit home exercise." It may feel a little silly at first, but practicing it will make it more likely that you will talk about your body in a more positive way. Think of which specific exercise you can do. I'd like to go around the room and ask each of you to share.

Have *each participant* state which affirmation exercise they are willing to do during the next week. Encourage them to write it down on the Self-Affirmation Exercise form to help them remember to do this activity.

Home Exercises (3 minutes)

■ Instruct group members to complete one of the positive body-talk exercises during the next week and fill-out the Self-Affirmation Exercise form in the workbook. Ask group members to e-mail you (and your co-leader) to talk about how it went.

■ Ask group members to write an e-mail letter to a teenage girl telling her how to avoid developing body image concerns. Ask the participants to send this letter to you (and your co-leader) as well.

Ask one participant to paraphrase the two exit home exercises to make sure that the directions are clear. Make sure that all participants have the facilitators' e-mail addresses.

Wrap-Up (10 minutes)

Well, this concludes the final session. Do you feel that this program has helped reduce your body image concerns? Have you noticed anything different about how you feel about your body?

Review any positive changes that participants might have noticed with regard to their body image concerns.

I want to thank each of your for signing up for this program. I really enjoyed your comments and participation in the group discussions. I hope that you feel it was worthwhile and that this experience helps you feel better about your body image now and far into the future. Please feel free to contact me if you have any setbacks or lingering concerns. Thanks again for your participation.

Self-Affirmation Exercise

Part of challenging body-related concerns involves talking about our bodies in a positive, rather than negative, way. We discussed some examples of this in the group, for instance, making a pledge to end complaints about your body or accepting compliments rather than objecting to them. Please choose an idea that we talked about, or one of your own, to practice over the next week, and let us know how it goes via email.

I am going to write down something positive about myself every time I catch myself thinking something negative about myself

---

Figure 5.1

Example of Completed Self-Affirmation Exercise Form

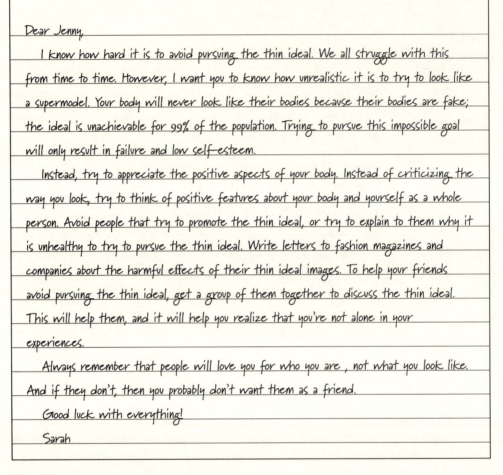

Letter to Adolescent Girl

Please write another letter to an adolescent girl telling her how to avoid developing body image concerns. Use any of the information you have learned in these session, and any additional ways you may think of on your own. The goal is to help her understand the different things she can do, say, avoid, or learn that will help her develop or maintain a positive body image.

Dear Jenny,

I know how hard it is to avoid pursuing the thin ideal. We all struggle with this from time to time. However, I want you to know how unrealistic it is to try to look like a supermodel. Your body will never look like their bodies because their bodies are fake; the ideal is unachievable for 99% of the population. Trying to pursue this impossible goal will only result in failure and low self-esteem.

Instead, try to appreciate the positive aspects of your body. Instead of criticizing the way you look, try to think of positive features about your body and yourself as a whole person. Avoid people that try to promote the thin ideal, or try to explain to them why it is unhealthy to try to pursue the thin ideal. Write letters to fashion magazines and companies about the harmful effects of their thin ideal images. To help your friends avoid pursuing the thin ideal, get a group of them together to discuss the thin ideal. This will help them, and it will help you realize that you're not alone in your experiences.

Always remember that people will love you for who you are, not what you look like. And if they don't, then you probably don't want them as a friend.

Good luck with everything!

Sarah

Figure 5.2

Example of Completed Letter to Adolescent Girl

If the group leaders decide to follow the Body Project sessions with the elective Healthy Weight sessions, they should read the following script:

The goal of these first four sessions was to help you appreciate the costs of pursuing the thin ideal promoted by our culture. The goal of the next four sessions is to help you make gradual and permanent lifestyle changes that will allow you to achieve the healthy ideal. We will start this module next week at the same time.

Elective Healthy
Weight Intervention

Part
2

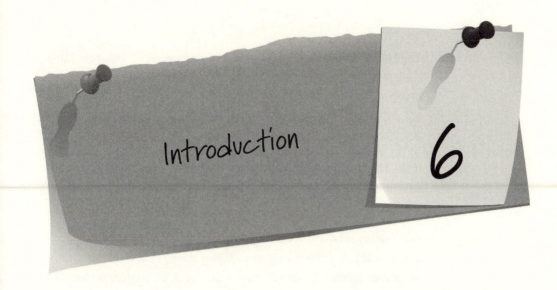

Introduction

6

As noted in chapter 1, previous trials have found that the Healthy Weight intervention, like the Body Project intervention, is also effective in reducing eating disorder symptoms and eating disorder risk factors. In addition, in one trial, the Healthy Weight intervention was even more effective than the Body Project intervention in reducing risk for future onset of eating disorder symptoms and risk for future onset of obesity. Accordingly, we have included the group leader script for the Healthy Weight intervention so that interested group leaders can offer this elective intervention following the Body Project intervention. Although no research has evaluated the effects of these interventions offered in sequence, both have produced positive intervention effects in trials conducted by multiple research groups (see chapter 1 for details).

If you do decide to offer the Healthy Weight intervention after delivery of the Body Project intervention, we recommend that the following rationale be offered to participants to justify the sequencing of the interventions:

Now that we have completed the Body Project intervention, which was intended to help you appreciate the costs of pursuing the thin ideal promoted by our culture, we would like to offer you the Healthy Weight intervention. This second intervention is designed to help you make gradual and permanent lifestyle changes that will allow you to achieve the healthy-ideal. The Healthy Weight intervention will give you tools to achieve and maintain a healthy body weight, which should further enhance body acceptance and help you avoid unhealthy weight-control behaviors.

The Healthy Weight intervention is based on a study performed at the University of Texas which suggested that young women who took a class on how to develop a healthy life-style showed marked improvements in body acceptance. They also were at a much lower risk for future onset of obesity and showed improvements in mood and interpersonal functioning.

If the Healthy Weight intervention is offered after the Body Project intervention, use the introduction shown above, rather than the original introduction, which is provided in chapter 7 (p. 74).

You should read the script that appears in italic font. Instructions appear in nonitalic font. Also, please try to follow the recommended time limits for each section, which will ensure that all of the content is covered.

Session 1

7

Materials Needed

- Flip chart or whiteboard and markers

- Attendance sheet

- Lifestyle Change Principles sheet

- Increasing Lifestyle Activity sheet

- Food Record form

- Exercise Record form

Session Outline

- Make introductions

- Provide a definition of the healthy ideal

- Define and discuss the concept of caloric intake and output

- Work with participants to help them implement healthy changes to their diet and exercise behaviors

- Assign home exercises

Overview

The focus of session 1 is on providing an overview of the program and on introducing participants to each other and orienting them to the rules and expectations of the group. In addition, in session I participants are asked to implement healthy changes to their diet and physical activity level.

Introduction (5 minutes)

At the start of the first session, welcome the members of the group and provide a brief description of the program.

Thanks for joining us. All of you decided to participate in these groups because of your body image concerns—a common concern. This intervention is based on a study performed at the University of Texas which suggested that young women who took a class on how to develop a healthy lifestyle showed marked improvements in body acceptance. They also were at a much lower risk for future onset of obesity and showed improvements in mood and interpersonal functioning.

Next, introduce yourself and the coleader (if applicable) to the group. Introductions include name, professional status, and personal information (e.g., something interesting or unique about yourself). Ask the group members to introduce themselves. This is an opportunity for you to break the ice and help participants feel comfortable discussing personal thoughts and experiences.

Let's start by getting to know each other better. Can each of you tell us your name, your year in school, and something interesting or unique about you?

Voluntary Commitment and Overview (5 minutes)

After the introduction has been completed, present the rationale for this intervention and ask the group members if they are willing to voluntarily commit to participating in the class.

The idea behind this class is that we can fine tune our energy balance on a permanent basis and develop a better relationship with food and body ac-

ceptance. The goal is to reach a balance that will permit you to stop obsessing about food and dieting and achieve a lasting healthy weight. We will use proven behavioral principles to achieve this aim because many people find it difficult to make lifestyle changes. This will help you feel better about your body and result in improved health. This intervention is also simple and can be easily incorporated into your busy life.

In addition, this program is based on the idea that by committing to these healthy lifestyle changes, you gain greater control over body shape, which should also help you feel better about your body. Finally, we deliver this intervention in a group format so that you can provide support for each other regarding body image issues.

Are you willing to give this a try?

Go around the room and have each participant say publicly that they are willing to actively participate. It is important to solicit verbal commitment to engage in the sessions and activities because this increases the level of investment in the group. Once group members express their commitment to the class, provide them with a verbal outline of the program (see table 7.1).

Confidentiality

It is important to discuss the issue of confidentiality with the group, as personal details of some of the group members' lives may be revealed during the course of the program. Additionally, when this intervention

---

Table 7.1 Program Outline

---

1. Differentiate the healthy-ideal from the thin-ideal.

2. Introduce the concept of reaching an energy balance.

3. Work with each of you to fine-tune your energy balance so you can achieve body satisfaction and lasting weight control.

4. Help you to generate ideas about how to eat healthfully and incorporate exercise into your daily lives in a way that is sustainable for the long term.

---

is conducted in settings such as high schools or sororities, there may be participants in the group who know each other or may come into contact outside of the group. It is critical that participants, particularly adolescents, feel confident that anything they share will not be repeated to anyone outside of the group in order to facilitate their discussion of personal experiences that may be embarrassing or sensitive.

While we are going through the different parts of this class, some of us will probably reveal some personal details about our lives. This can be hard to do when we aren't sure if we can trust that others won't repeat what we've said. So we ask that everything said in our group remains completely confidential. Can everyone agree to this?

Attendance

Stress the importance of attending all classes. Each session builds on skills and concepts discussed in the previous session, and group members should be encouraged to attend each session. You may find that arranging a make-up session for those who are unable to attend is helpful for achieving retention. However, attendance at regular sessions should be strongly encouraged, as participation in the group likely fosters group cohesion and support.

It is also important that everyone attends all four sessions of this group. If for some reason you need to miss a session, please let me (or coleader) know as soon as you know that you are going to be gone. We will need to schedule a make-up session with you before the next regular group session so you will be caught up with everyone else.

We recommend calling or e-mailing participants the day before each session to remind participants of the session and to remind them to bring any assignments that are due. If a participant must miss a session for any reason, schedule a brief (15 minute) individual make-up session to discuss key points from the session so that the participant will be caught up for the next session. Ask them to complete the home exercises before the next session. These make-up sessions are an important key to the success of this intervention; they send a clear message to the participants that it

Attendance Sheet

Record names of participants and check if they attend each session. This will assist you in knowing who to contact for an individual make-up session, if they miss a session.

Names of participants in the group:	Session 1	Session 2	Session 3	Session 4
1. _____	•	•	•	•
2. _____	•	•	•	•
3. _____	•	•	•	•
4. _____	•	•	•	•
5. _____	•	•	•	•
6. _____	•	•	•	•
7. _____	•	•	•	•
8. _____	•	•	•	•
9. _____	•	•	•	•
10. _____	•	•	•	•
11. _____	•	•	•	•
12. _____	•	•	•	•

is important for them to attend each session. If the participant anticipates missing more than one session at the outset, they should be scheduled for another group if possible because the group context may be an
important element in helping facilitate attitudinal change. We have included an attendance sheet because it helps group leaders know who has
missed particular sessions.

At this point in the session, you should initiate a discussion of the healthy ideal. Pose questions to the group and promote participation and collaboration on their responses.

First, we need to distinguish between the thin ideal and the healthy ideal.

What are the features of the ultraslender ideal espoused by the fashion industry and the media?

The likely answer to this question is extremely thin. Spend no more than a minute on this to avoid critiquing the thin ideal.

How does this contrast to what might be called the healthy ideal?

The healthy ideal is a reasonably slender body, but one that has muscles and fat as well. Each is natural and serves important functions. Explain that it is possible to be healthy and yet still not meet our society's ultra-slender ideal.

Many women have body image concerns that are rooted in a pursuit of the thin ideal, which is unrealistic and is not healthy. What are some of the advantages of aspiring to a healthy ideal?

Spend the most time discussing the following benefits. Verbalizing the merits of striving for a healthy weight helps increase participants' investment in pursuing the healthy ideal.

■ Health benefits (longer life, fewer illnesses such as cancer, fewer injuries; higher quality of life, freedom of mobility, increased fertility, fewer birth complications)

■ Social benefits (more social acceptance, easier to meet new friends; easier to find dates, higher marriage rates, easier to get jobs, higher salaries, higher social class)

■ Emotional benefits (less obsessions about weight and eating, better able to focus on school and studies; lower rates of depression, higher self-esteem and self-confidence, general well-being, more energy, greater productivity).

Explain to the group that this program will teach the skills necessary to make lasting lifestyle changes.

Many people find it difficult to reach the healthy ideal because of an incomplete understanding of the causes of weight gain and because they lack the skills to make lasting behavior change. An improved understanding of these factors will help you achieve a healthier weight, which will give you more energy, self-confidence, and greater body acceptance. This group will help you learn to make these behavioral changes and will provide a source of support as you incorporate them into your daily life.

Energy Balance

Discuss the concept of energy balance and how caloric intake and output play an important role in determining body weight. This is a simple concept, but many individuals fail to consider both sides of the energy equation. Often, people feel discouraged about changing their shape or weight because they believe that weight is primarily genetically determined. Acknowledging the contribution of genetic factors while stressing that behavior is a more important determinant of weight can help bolster participants' self-efficacy for achieving change. Group leaders should be sensitive to the possibility that some group members may want to *gain* weight and thus emphasize achieving and maintaining a healthy weight—whatever that means for each individual.

Body weight is a function of caloric intake and output. If you consume more calories than you use, you gain weight; if you consume less than you use, you lose weight. If you want to maintain weight, you need to balance this equation. Thus, achieving a healthy weight is simply a function of decreasing your intake of the foods highest in fat and increasing your caloric expenditure. This is the premise of this class, and we will focus on how to fine tune your energy balance. You need to consume just enough calories to meet your needs and not more.

Some of you may think that your weight is completely determined by genetic factors. However, genetics actually play a limited role in determining body weight compared to lifestyle behaviors. You simply need to find an intake and output balance that helps you attain a healthy weight given your genes and metabolism.

We'll therefore spend time examining your caloric intake and output, with the goal of making slight alterations that will allow you to reach and maintain a healthy body weight.

It is important to note that these changes will be individualized. Some of you will need to reduce your intake of high fat foods, others will need to increase their intake of fruits and vegetables, and others may need to increase their intake of high-energy foods, such as complex carbohydrates. Others may need to reduce or stop drinking alcohol or using illegal substances, such as marijuana (which can often lead to overeating and poor food choices). Some may decide that they want to avoid situations that are high-risk times for overeating, such as late night trips to fast-food restaurants.

Energy Balance versus Dieting

Explain to the group that the Healthy Weight program is not about dieting; it is about making a lifestyle change and committing to a healthy way of life.

Please note that we are not suggesting you diet. Dieting refers to time-limited constraints on caloric intake intended to counteract the effects of overeating. Many diets involve deprivation, and people typically go on and off diets. Although diets are popular and sometimes effective in the short term, almost all people regain the weight they lost while on a diet.

Instead, we suggest you make smaller, permanent changes to your caloric intake and output that you can maintain for the rest of your life. This approach represents a lifestyle commitment. It involves making healthy habits a part of day-to-day life. Can you commit to this lifestyle approach?

By definition, the energy balance approach ensures that you are not deprived; rather, you are simply trying to find a more appropriate level of caloric intake. Note that you will lose weight even if you eat the number of calories that you need to maintain a healthy body size. This is because you need more energy to keep an overweight body warm and supplied with blood.

Define the concept of caloric input.

A calorie is a measure of energy, which refers to both the energy potential in a food and how much energy your body needs to function. (One calorie is the energy needed to raise the temperature of one gram of water one degree centigrade).

When your basic energy requirements are met, the body stores excess calories as fat.

At this point, highlight five principles that will help participants improve their dietary intake. Write down each principle on a flip-chart or whiteboard as it is discussed.

1.   Substitutions

Substitution refers to replacing foods with a lot of calories with lower calorie alternatives—foods that still make you feel full and satisfied. For example, you can replace ice cream with frozen yogurt or sorbet. You'll still feel satisfied, but with fewer calories. Choose skim milk instead of whole or 2%, mustard or low-fat mayo instead of regular mayo, etcetera. The idea is to replace high-fat foods with lower fat foods or high-sugar foods with lower sugar foods.

Can you name what you suspect is the highest calorie food of your weekly diet and name a lower calorie substitute? I'll start, so we are all disclosing. I enjoy eating (pick your own examples).

Write down example substitutions to help participants remember these ideas. Any misperceptions that participants have should be corrected. For example, many low-fat versions of popular foods (such as cookies), are still highly caloric due to extremely high sugar content.

2.   Start your meal right

Another aspect of lowering caloric density is to start your meals with foods that have high water content (like fruit, vegetables, salad, or soup). This is a healthy way to feel full faster, and it ensures that the calories you are filling up on are healthier. You will be less likely to overeat if you start it with a healthier but filling food because you will feel full while eating less. Foods with a lot of water content are good choices to accomplish this. Drinking a lot of water before a meal does not have the same effect, however.

What other healthy foods could you start a meal with to help you from overeating high-calorie foods during mealtimes?

Write down these ideas.

3. Smaller portion sizes

The next principle to help change your diet is smaller portion sizes. If you are going to eat something high in calories, fat, or sugar, eat a smaller portion. This can be hard based on habits of grabbing a large plate or bowl and filling it to capacity. One way to change this habit is to use smaller dishes and utensils.

For example, instead of a large cereal bowl for ice cream, you could use a coffee cup. Instead of a pint glass of juice, use a 6-ounce glass. You can still have the higher calorie foods, just try to eat them less often, and eat less of them when you do.

What are other ways to decrease your portion sizes?

Write down these ideas.

More examples for achieving smaller serving sizes are:

■   Never opt for supersize servings.

■   Start with small servings at meals and get more if not full. People are more likely to eat everything they are served, even if they feel full without finishing the serving.

■   Don't eat out of the container. Take a small serving instead.

■   When eating out at a restaurant that has large portion sizes, ask the server to immediately box up one-half of the meal.

4. Less variety

Instead of eating four different types of food at a meal—for example, meat, vegetable, potato, and bread, limit your meal to a couple of food items. This will help you reach that full feeling faster and help you refrain from over- eating. However, it is best to NOT cut out vegetables or fruits. Remember that those are higher in water content and make you feel full with fewer calo- ries. Instead, cut foods like starches or carbohydrates (potatoes and bread) or less healthy foods.

What are some foods you would be willing to cut from your favorite meals?

Write down these ideas.

5.   Healthier food environment

To help you reduce your intake of foods high calorie foods, don't keep them around. If you don't have cookies in your cupboard when you're looking for something to snack on, you're more likely to settle for something healthier that you do have, or nothing at all if you're not really hungry. In essence, don't set yourself up for failure—if the food is there, you will eat it!

This can be tough when vending machines and snack shops are around. We suggest that you select routes around town or campus that do not bring you past tempting snack shops or vending machines. You can also leave your money at home, so you are not tempted to purchase snacks.

If your group is composed of college students, suggest that they talk to their roommates or housemates about helping each other keep only healthy foods around. If your group is composed of high school students, suggest that they talk to their parents and siblings about keeping only healthy foods in the house.

What ways can you give yourself a healthier food environment or avoid the less healthy ones?

Write down these ideas.

Once all ideas have been written down, continue the discussion by asking participants if they can come up with ways to change their diets this week to make them healthier.

Can each of you come up with one way that you will change your diet this week to make it healthier? Use the principles we just talked about for ideas. We are not calling for radical changes in your diets; we only want to fine tune your energy balance. The important point is that YOU get to make the decision of what, and when, you change your eating.

Go around the room and make sure everyone commits to one healthy change to their dietary intake. Get public commitments. Encourage small changes if a participant attempts to make a change that you think will be too extreme and therefore unlikely to be achieved.

Lifestyle Change Principles

Five Principles to Help You Change your Diet

Please think of examples of ways you can implement each principle into your own daily life and diet. Try to make these examples specific to your own lifestyle.

1) Substitutions:

   Instead of snacking on regular chips, I can eat baked chips.

2) Start Your Meal Right:

   I will have a salad with dinner, and eat the salad first.

   I will get vegetable soup with lunch, and start with the soup.

3) Smaller Portion Sizes:

   I will look at the serving sizes on the food I eat, and notice if I usually eat more than one serving.

   When I eat ice cream, I'll use a coffee cup rather than a bowl.

   Instead of sitting down with a whole bag of pretzels or chips, I'll put a serving of them in a bowl and eat only that amount.

4) Less Variety:

   At dinner, instead of having pasta, bread, a salad, and a soda, I can have just salad and pasta, and drink water with lemon.

   When I go to the sandwich shop, I can skip the chips and cookie and just get a sandwich and a refreshing low-calorie drink.

   When I go to a party or a buffet where lots of different food is available, I can pick just 2 or 3 of my favorite foods rather than lots of different items.

5) Healthier Food Environment:

   I will buy single servings of my favorite delicious fried tortilla chips rather than the whole bag, so it won't sit around my room waiting to be eaten!

   I can't pass by the cinnamon roll shop without needing a cinnamon roll, so I'll take another route to where I'm going.

Figure 7.1
Example of Completed Lifestyle Change Principles

Three Principles to Help You Exercise More

Just as you did for the principles about eating healthier, please think of examples of ways you can implement the exercise principles into your own daily life.

1) Add Exercise to your Schedule:

> I will schedule 30 minutes for walking or jogging on Tuesday and Thursday mornings, when my classes don't start till noon.
>
> I will join the local hiking club and go hiking on the weekends.

2) Incidental Exercise:

> I can get off the bus two stops before school and walk the rest of the way.
>
> I will walk to the convenience store a few blocks away, rather than driving.
>
> If I'm a little early to class, I can explore the building rather than sitting in the hall outside the classroom.

3) Think Flexibly about Exercise:

> Going out dancing with friends on the weekend is exercise! As long as I actually get onto the dance floor.
>
> I can play Frisbee on campus between classes with friends.
>
> I love to go shopping at the mall, and I can walk around and explore different stores to get in more walking.

Figure 7.1 *continued*

> *It is particularly important for you to develop healthy habits regarding dietary intake at this point in your life. You are becoming an independent adult and have started or may soon start living on your own. For many of you, this will be the first time that you are solely responsible for what you eat. This means that the habits you develop now may be with you for the rest of your life.*
>
> *It's important to distinguish deprivation from balanced eating. If you have slowly been gaining weight over time, you have been taking in an excess of calories, and you should balance the energy equation. This is different from being deprived, which is eating less than your body needs. What we are asking you to do is cut out excess intake.*

Define the concept of caloric output.

The other side of the energy equation is output, which means exercise. Exercise can involve lifestyle behaviors, such as biking to school or work and using the stairs. Exercise can also involve more formal exercise such as running, playing volleyball, or aerobics. Not only does regular exercise help balance the energy equation by using more calories, it also increases your metabolism.

At this point, highlight the three principles that will help participants improve their exercise habits. Write down each principle on a flip-chart or whiteboard as it is discussed.

It can be difficult to increase physical activity, but exercise is essential if you want to stay in shape and keep your body healthy. Exercise also keeps your caloric intake more in balance with your caloric output (the energy you use through physical activity). Many people feel like they don't have time to exercise or they're too tired after a long day at work or school. Just as we did with healthier eating, we have principles that will make it easier to make small but important changes in your exercise habits.

Emphasize that regular exercise is the best predictor of long-term maintenance of weight loss.

1. Add exercise to your schedule

Pick a time of day that you will be most likely to exercise, and pick something that you enjoy and do it! Scheduling exercise with a friend can help motivate you, but don't give up if your friend can't make it one day. Don't tell yourself you'll work out at the gym for 30 minutes a day if you hate the gym. Just take a walk around your neighborhood. Play a sport if it seems fun. There are sports teams that are at all different levels, which can be a great way to meet people and exercise more. Even if it's not organized, you can get a few friends together and go play basketball or go for a hike. Explore town by riding a bike around. It is best to eventually commit to an hour of exercise a day.

What are some things you can do to exercise more that would be fun?

Write ideas on the board.

2. Incidental exercise

Think of exercise that you could work into your daily routine. If you need to reach an upper level of a building, take the stairs rather than the elevator. If you normally drive or take the bus to school or work, ride a bike or walk. When walking to your destination, leave a little early and take a less direct path to get there. If you must drive, park farther away from the building than you typically would. All of these things takes just a few minutes more and adds exercise to your day.

What are some forms of incidental exercise you can think of that would fit with your daily routines?

Write ideas on the board.

3. Think flexibly about exercise

Exercise can happen anywhere at any time. If you think you don't have time to exercise because you can't go out and run or work out at the gym, rethink what exercise is. If you're waiting for a plane at the airport, take a walk with your bags around the airport instead of waiting at the gate. Just because your morning is filled with traveling, you can take the opportunities you have to walk a little more, stretch, and get your muscles moving. Walking to class, biking downtown, doing yard work or house cleaning—these are all things that you have to do, and they all involve exercise.

Instruct participants to turn to the Increasing Lifestyle Activity sheet in the workbook.

The Increasing Lifestyle Activity sheet in your workbook has some suggestions for how to implement some of these principles into your regular routine.

What are some activities that you do that would also count as exercise, and what are some times when you could exercise rather than sitting around?

Write ideas on the board.

Making these changes will require some effort at first, but if you make small steps, they can become part of a new routine.

Once all ideas have been written down, continue the discussion by asking participants to come up with ways of increasing their physical activity.

We would like each of you to develop an individualized plan for increasing physical activity. For some we will recommend beginning regular exercise, whereas for others we may recommend cross-training to minimize the risk of injury, and for others we may recommend a decrease in overall exercise level if it is very high.

Can each of you commit to one increase in your physical activity that you can maintain? It may be as simple as taking a 20-minute walk each day, or it may be more ambitious, such as jogging a few miles every other day. The choice is yours—we are just here to support you in reaching your goals.

What will each of you do to exercise more?

Go around the room, getting public commitment to one activity from each participant. Some participants find it helpful to set an exercise goal, such as doing 10K race or swimming 1 mile.

If a participant is already exercising more than 2 hours a day, encourage cross-training or a potential reduction in overall exercise.

This is an individually tailored program—it all comes down to what will work for you. On this note, it is important to consider your weight gain trajectory of your current input/output level. If you are slowly inching up the scale, only slight alterations are necessary. If you are gaining weight rapidly, more significant alterations may be required.

It is also important to remember that this approach will only work is if you are candid about your eating and exercise. There is clear evidence that some people under-report caloric intake and overreport exercise. There is no way this group can be helpful to you if you are not honest regarding your eating and exercise behaviors. Part of what we will do here is talk about what difficulties arise in making these changes, and we will help you come up with ways to address these problems.

Home Exercises (5 minutes)

When assigning home exercises, it is important to provide verbal instructions on how to use each form. You should also remind participants that attendance is very important. Collect e-mail addresses and phone

Food Record-Week 1

Please keep track of the food you eat for 2 weekdays and 1 weekend day over the course of this week. This will help you to become aware of what you are putting in your body. You may photocopy this page or download multiple Food Records at the Treatments *ThatWork*™ Web site (http://www.oup.com/us/ttw).

Please record one healthy change you're making to your food intake this week:

Have only one healthy snack after dinner.

Weekday #1

Time	Food	Amount
7:30 am	Yogurt Cashews Watermelon Tea	8 oz. 1/4 cup 2 cups cubed 1 cup with 1 Tbsp. milk
11:00 am	Banana Almonds Herb tea	1 medium 1/4 cup 1 cup
12:30 pm	Sandwich Baby carrots Dark chocolate Coffee	2 Tbsp. egg salad, 1/2 cup spinach, 2 slices bread 7 1 square (1/2 oz.) 1 cup with 1 tsp. sugar, 1 Tbsp. milk
3:00 pm	Peach Granola bar	1 large 1
6:00 pm	Salad Salad dressing Grilled cheese sandwich Herb tea	1 cup lettuce, 1/4 cup garbanzo beans, few shredded carrots, few cherry tomatoes 2 Tbsp. 2 slices bread, 2 slices cheese, 2 Tbsp. butter 12 oz. with 1 tsp. sugar
9:00 pm	Multigrain cereal Banana Chopped pecans Soymilk	1 cup 1/2 medium 2 Tbsp. 1 cup

Figure 7.2

Example of Completed Food Record- Week 1

Exercise Record - Week 1

Please write down each time you exercise for at least 20 minutes this week. This can be planned exercise, like jogging, or incidental exercise, like walking across campus to your classes. You may photocopy this page or download multiple Exercise Records at the Treatments *ThatWork*™ Web site (http://www.oup.com/us/ttw).

Please record one healthy change you're making to your exercise this week:

Add strength-training exercises twice a week for twenty minutes.

Day	Type of Exercise	Amount of Time
Thurs 8/17	Upper-body exercises with weights	30 min
Fri 8/18	Jogging	30 min
Fri 8/18	Salsa dancing	1 hour
Sun 8/20	Cleaning house	1 hour
Mon 8/21	Walking to & from classes	20 min
Tues 8/22	Jogging	30 min
Tues 8/22	Ab & back exercises	20 min
Wed 8/23	Walking to & from classes	20 min

Figure 7.3

Example of Completed Exercise Record - Week 1

numbers so that you can remind people about the home exercises and importance of attending each session.

■ Instruct participants to make one healthy change to their diet and one healthy change to their physical activity in the coming week.

■ Ask participants to begin keeping a food record for 2 weekdays and 1 weekend day using the Food Record form in the workbook. Introduce the form using the following dialogue:

Also, please keep a food record for 2 weekdays and 1 weekend day using the form in your workbook. Record everything you eat and provide a general index of portion size, as well as the general time of day each was eaten. Try to record after every eating episode, because we forget otherwise. Please record the one healthy change to your diet that you are going to make. Bring these forms next time because we will use them to make further healthy dietary changes.

■ Ask participants to begin keeping an exercise record for at least 2 weekdays and 1 weekend day using the Exercise Record form in the workbook. Introduce the form using the following dialogue:

For your second home exercise, we would like you to keep an exercise log using the form in your workbook. Please write down every time you exercise for at least 20 minutes and record the other lifestyle changes you made. Please also record the one healthy increase to your physical activity that you are going to make. Bring these forms next time because we will use them to make further lifestyle changes.

Session 2

8

Materials Needed

- Tips for Eating Out
- Physical Activity Fact sheet
- Top 10 Reasons to Pursue a Healthy Lifestyle list
- Food Record form
- Exercise Record form

Session Outline

- Review the benefits of achieving the healthy ideal
- Review home exercises from previous session
- Continue to work with participants to help them implement further healthy changes to their diet and exercise programs
- Assign home exercises

Motivational Enhancement (5 minutes)

Remind participants of the benefits of achieving the healthy ideal that were discussed at the last session. This helps reinforce motivation to make lasting changes to dietary intake and activity levels.

Can any of you remember some of these benefits?

- Health benefits (longer life, less illness such as cancer, fewer injuries, higher quality of life, easier to get pregnant, fewer birth complications)

- Social benefits (more acceptance, higher marriage rates, easier to get jobs, higher salaries, higher social class)

- Emotional benefits (less obsessions about weight and eating, lower rates of depression, greater self-confidence, feeling better in general, more energy, greater productivity)

Can each of you voice the most important benefit of achieving the healthy ideal for you?

Again, this intervention is based on the following ideas:

1. *Using behavioral techniques to fine tune our energy balance through healthy lifestyle changes will result in body acceptance. These changes will be individual in nature and are under your control.*

2. *Committing to these healthy lifestyle changes will make you feel more in control of your body, which will make you feel better about it.*

3. *The group will serve as an important source of support for each of you.*

Healthy Dietary Change (15 minutes)

Review with the group the importance of making slight decreases in caloric intake to achieve a better balance between caloric input and output.

I want to recap the principles we talked about last week.

- *We talked about substitution—replacing high calorie foods with lower calorie foods that will make you feel just as satisfied.*

■ *We talked about starting out right—eating a food with high water content as a first course so that you'll feel full and not eat as much of the foods that are higher in calories.*

■ *We talked about using smaller portion sizes to reduce caloric intake.*

■ *We talked about making a healthier food environment for yourself—keeping your living environment free of unhealthy foods and changing how often you frequent places that sell or serve unhealthy foods.*

I would like to hear how each of you did with regard to the change you planned on making to your diet, whether you used these principles, and whether you encountered any problems with the change plan.

Have each participant discuss how the change plan worked last week. If they did not make the behavior change, briefly assess what happened and brainstorm solutions. Ask the participant to discuss a time when they planned to implement their elected behavior change and determine where they got off track (e.g., a particular situation, thought, emotion). Let group members provide input to each other.

Apply principles of behavior modification when possible (e.g., making small, observable changes, making the behavior change before participating in an enjoyable activity, reinforcing new healthy behaviors).

If this program is being offered to college students, it might be useful to cover the following points:

Eating healthfully in the dormitory environment can be particularly challenging. First, there is a limited selection of healthy foods in the cafeterias. Second, it is often difficult to avoid high-fat foods that are displayed next to the lower fat healthy foods. Third, the fact that the dorm café is open until late in the evening may make it tempting to go there and overeat. At other times, you may not have access to the cafeteria, which might make it more likely that you order unhealthy food for delivery, go out for fast food, or frequent convenience stores.

There are a few things you can do to overcome these barriers. Make sure low-fat snack foods such as pretzels and fruit are in your backpack, dorm room, or kitchen so you reach for them instead. Limit your time in the cafeteria— leave when you're done eating, and choose another place to hang out with friends. Make sure you have consumed three full meals in the cafeterias while they are open each day.

Food Record Review and Further Healthy Dietary Change (10 minutes)

We asked you to keep a food record so that we can see how we might best balance your energy equation. Based on your food records, can you identify a second change you can make to improve your diet in the coming week?

Go around the room and get a public commitment to one healthy change from each participant.

I want to reiterate that you should not go long periods without eating. Such caloric deprivation often triggers overeating and is thus self-defeating. I also want to reiterate that the choice is yours to make—we are just here to support you in reaching your goals.

Another way to improve your dietary intake is to be more conscious when you're eating out. This will be especially important to those who eat at campus cafeterias your first year of college. The Tips for Eating Out sheet in your workbook has suggestions on how to approach eating out and eating in campus cafeterias.

Instruct participants to turn to the Tips for Eating Out sheet in the workbook.

We also want to encourage you to focus on shape rather than weight. Weight is just a proxy measure of shape and one that does not differentiate increases in muscle (which weighs more) from increases in fat. You may be moving toward a healthy ideal but show slight increases in weight. Use the way your clothes fit instead of the scale to provide feedback.

It is also important that you not engage in radical weight control efforts, such as vomiting or laxative use. These behaviors are not effective in losing weight, they can cause medical problems, and they have been found to predict onset of obesity.

Smoking to control weight is also a bad idea because smoking leads to lasting health problems and makes exercise more difficult. Also, smoking is not a sustainable method of weight control, and most people gain weight when they quit.

Review with the group the importance of increasing exercise to help achieve a better balance between caloric intake and output.

I want to recap the exercise principles we talked about last week.

■ *We talked about scheduling time to exercise.*

■ *We talked about selecting a type of exercise that you enjoy.*

■ *We talked about increasing your incidental exercise (such as walking to school).*

■ *We talked about thinking flexibly about exercise (such as doing yard work).*

Were you able to make the planned changes to your exercise routine? What did you do? Did you use one of the principles? What are some of the things that make these types of changes difficult?

Go around the room and troubleshoot as necessary. If a participant did not complete her behavior change plan, assess what happened and brainstorm solutions. Let group members provide input for each other.

Apply principles of behavior modification when possible. For example, make exercise a social event by taking a walk with a friend. Suggest that participants get a friend to commit to exercising together on a regular basis. Come up with a back-up plan for exercising. For example, if a participant planned to run outside but it is raining that day, have an alternate plan ready, such as attending a Pilate's class. Make enjoyable activities contingent on exercise (e.g., you can only watch your favorite TV show if you exercised that day).

We should review some of the benefits of exercise. Do you recall some of the benefits we discussed?

Exercise

■ Increases heart and lung endurance

■ Increases muscular strength and endurance

■ Increases flexibility

- Decreases heart rate and blood pressure

- Decreases risk of osteoporosis

- Increases calorie burning

- Increases metabolic rate

- Helps manage stress

- Increases feeling of well-being

- Boosts hormones that can improve mood

- Enables mastery of a new skill

- Provides opportunities to meet people (at the gym or at the park, for example).

Increased exercise has additive benefits. Adding 60 minutes a day of light activity such as walking will reduce your risk of heart disease. Moderate activity such as biking or dancing for 30 minutes or more at least 4 days a week can help reduce elevated blood pressure. Vigorous activity such as running can provide even more protection from heart disease. The Physical Activity Fact sheet in your workbook details these benefits.

Instruct participants to turn to the Physical Activity Fact sheet in the workbook.

Exercise Record Review and Further Healthy Exercise Change (10 minutes)

We asked you to keep an exercise log so that we can take a closer look at your output to see how we might best increase your exercise. Based on this exercise record, can you identify a way to make a second improvement to your physical activity in the coming week?

Try to get participants to identify potential changes, but suggest changes if necessary. Get public commitment.

Here are some other ideas regarding ways to exercise more if participants have problems coming up with ways to increase exercise:

- Ride a bike to campus instead of driving.

- Make plans to go to the gym regularly at specific times and stick to it.

- Get an exercise partner to help you get going and keep you motivated.

- Register for an exercise class through the PE department.

- Don't view exercise as having to be done in one big chunk; split it up into smaller sessions.

- Take a 30-minute walk in a pleasant area in the morning or afternoon.

- Take the stairs to a class that's on a higher floor, or to your dorm room.

- Take a dance class.

- Get off the bus a few stops early and walk the rest of the way to campus.

- Write in your planner when you will work out and what you'll do, and keep it as you would any other appointment.

- Give yourself a reward, such as a new compact disc, if you meet your exercise goals for the week.

- Identify activities that you like to do and locations that you enjoy. Don't force yourself to work out in a way or place you dislike (e.g., you may not like the gym at the busiest time of day).

- Plan ahead for busy times like midterms and final exams, and make a workout schedule that you can maintain during those times.

Home Exercises (5 minutes)

- Instruct each group member to make one additional healthy change to their diet and one additional healthy change to their physical activity plan in the coming week.

- Group members should continue to keep food and exercise records over the next week.

- Ask group members to list 10 reasons to pursue the healthy ideal that are personally meaningful to each of them using the Top 10 Reasons to Pursue a Healthy Lifestyle list in the workbook.

Top 10 Reasons to Pursue a Healthy Lifestyle

Please come up with your top 10 reasons for pursuing a healthy lifestyle. You can use some of the reasons we discussed in the group (such as decreased risk for disease), and also come up with some of your own.

1) Have more energy.

2) Reduce stress.

3) Make friends doing new outdoor activities.

4) Reduce risk for disease later in life.

5) Increase muscle strength and cardiovascular health.

6) Be able to jog in a 10K.

7) Try new healthy foods.

8) Have a reason to reward myself when I achieve health goals.

9) Stop using unhealthy ways of controlling calories.

10) Learn new physical activities like snowboarding.

Figure 8.1

Example of Completed Top 10 Reasons to Pursue a Healthy Lifestyle

Materials Needed

- Fruits and Vegetables/Benefits by Color handout
- Exercise and Caloric Expenditure Fact sheet
- Food Record form
- Exercise Record form

Session Outline

- Review benefits of achieving the healthy ideal
- Review home exercises from previous session
- Continue to work with participants to help them implement further healthy changes to their diet and exercise behaviors
- Assign home exercises

Motivational Enhancement (5 minutes)

We have discussed the benefits of attaining a healthy ideal, which include longer life, decreased injury and illness, greater social acceptance, improved employment options, higher salary, elevated marriage rates, and greater self-confidence.

Is anyone willing to read your top two personal reasons for pursuing the healthy ideal that you generated for home exercise?

Have you begun to notice any improvements in your own life? Do you feel better about your relationship with food and your body? Do you feel more self-assured? Do you feel better about your body?

Encourage participants to discuss the benefits of making these changes.

Healthy Dietary Change (15 minutes)

Last week we discussed the importance of making slight decreases in your caloric intake to achieve a better balance between caloric input and output.

We also discussed several principles for changing dietary intake, including substituting lower calorie foods for higher calorie foods, starting meals with food that is high in water content, using smaller portion sizes, and changing your food environment.

Were you able to make the planned adjustment to your intake? Which principles did you use?

What are some of the things that make these types of changes difficult? How did you overcome them (or if you didn't, how could you overcome them in the future)?

Have each participant discuss how the change plan worked last week. If they did not make the behavior change, briefly assess what happened and brainstorm solutions. Let group members provide input to each other.

Apply principles of behavior modification when possible (e.g., making small, observable changes, making the behavior change before participating in an enjoyable activity, reinforcing changes).

Some of you may find that you are eating in response to emotions. For instance, you may be eating because you are stressed by your classes, because you are feeling rejected by a partner, or because you are feeling lonely in a new place. It will be important for you to identify these emotional triggers of overeating and use new coping strategies for dealing with these feelings. For example, rather than going out for ice cream when you are feeling lonely, perhaps you could visit a new friend or call an old friend or a family member.

Group leaders should help participants identify problematic emotional eating and generate alternative strategies for dealing with these emotions. Participants may also want to carefully record the emotional state that preceded any overeating so they can identify emotional triggers for overeating.

Food Record Review and Further Healthy Dietary Change (10 minutes)

We asked you to keep a food record so that we can see how we might best balance your energy equation. Based on your food records, can you identify another change you can make to improve your diet in the coming week?

Go around the room and get a public commitment to one healthy change for each participant.

One great way to decrease your caloric intake and add lots of vitamins, minerals, and fiber to your diet is by eating plenty of fruits and vegetables. The American Dietetic Association recommends five servings of fruits and vegetables per day. It's easy to replace less healthy foods with fruits and vegetables. For example, instead of having cookies or candy as a snack or for dessert, try having fruit and yogurt or granola. Have a salad or vegetable soup or extra veggies with meals to help you to feel full and to add nutrients. Can anyone think of other ways to incorporate more fruits and vegetables into your diet?

Instruct participants to turn to the Fruits and Vegetables/Benefits by Color handout in the workbook.

This page lists more than 100 different fruits and vegetables. Changing your eating habits might mean introducing new foods into your diet that you've never tried. A new, healthy food might turn out to be a good substitute for an unhealthy food.

Notice that the fruits and vegetables are categorized into different color categories and that each category has specific health benefits. You all deserve to have the health benefits listed on this handout. Let's go through these benefits.

Review the health benefits listed on the handout.

We encourage you to recognize all of the positive facets of yourself in addition to your physical health, including your humor, wit, intelligence, and talents. We hope this will make you more willing to take care of yourself by making healthy lifestyle changes. Can each of you share two non–body-related qualities that you like about yourself?

Remember to appreciate your efforts. You're doing something very important for yourself by coming to these classes and making these changes. Sometimes it's difficult to remember the progress we've made when we're focused on moving toward our goals. One way to appreciate your efforts is to reward yourself for your accomplishments. Let's list some small non-food rewards that you can give yourself for achieving your healthy dietary and exercise change goals. These don't have to take a lot of time or cost a lot of money. I'll start.

Sample rewards:

- Take a long bubble bath

- Go hear some live music

- Buy yourself a new compact disc

- Treat yourself to a book or favorite magazine

- Watch a favorite television show

- Purchase some new exercise clothing

- Get a massage

Healthy Exercise Change (15 minutes)

Review with the group the importance of increasing exercise to help achieve a better balance between caloric intake and output.

Last week we also talked about the importance of increasing your exercise level to help you achieve a better balance between your intake and output.

We also discussed principles that may help you increase your physical activity, including scheduling time for exercise, selected exercise that you enjoy, engaging in incidental exercise, and thinking flexibly about ways to exercise.

Were you able to make the planned changes to your exercise routine? What did you do? Did you use one of the principles? What are some of the things that make these types of changes difficult?

Go around the room and troubleshoot as necessary. If they did not complete their behavior change plan, assess what happened and brainstorm solutions. Let group members provide input for each other.

Apply principles of behavior modification when possible , such as rewarding yourself for making the healthy change in your exercise routine.

I want to talk a little more about exercise. Sometimes people get bored with their exercise programs because they only do one type of exercise or they select a type of exercise that they don't enjoy. These are major reasons that people stop exercising.

Let's brainstorm as many types of exercise as we can think of. I'll write them down on the board, and I'd like you to write them down to keep as a reference. You can look at this list when you want more variety in your exercise routine.

Get suggestions and write them on the board.

I'd also like you to review the Exercise and Caloric Expenditure Fact sheet in the workbook so that you can have an idea of how many calories you are burning while you are doing these activities. This list may contain some activities we normally wouldn't think of as exercise, but as this sheet demonstrates, they are activities that burn lots of calories.

It's also important to have a balance between cardiovascular exercise, strength training, and flexibility. These are three important components of fitness that should be balanced in an exercise routine. Each component contributes to overall health in its own unique way, and all are equally important. Let's go through this list that we've generated and classify each exercise as cardio, strength, or flexibility.

Go through the list and let participants classify each; help as necessary.

Exercise Record Review and Further Healthy Exercise Change (10 minutes)

We asked you to keep an exercise log so that we can take a closer look at your physical activity to see how we might best help balance your energy equation.

Looking at your exercise record, can you see which of the three components of exercise you should add—cardiovascular, strength training, and flexibility exercise?

For the next week, can each of you identify one way you can improve your exercise routine? You might consider adding the exercise component that is not currently well represented in your routine.

Go around the room and ask each participant how they plan to improve their exercise routine. Try to get participants to make the suggestion for changes to their exercise plan, but you can make suggestions if necessary. Get public commitment from each participant.

Home Exercises (5 minutes)

- Group members should continue to make one additional healthy change to their diet and one additional healthy change to their physical activity in the coming week.

- Group members should continue to keep food and exercise records over the next week and note barriers to making healthy changes.

Session Outline

- Review participants' progress up to this point

- Review home exercises from previous session

- Continue to work with participants to help them implement further healthy changes to their diet and exercise behaviors over the next 6 months

- Discuss relapse prevention

- Assign home exercise

Motivational Enhancement (5 minutes)

We have discussed the benefits of attaining a healthy ideal, which includes longer life, decreased injury and illness, greater social acceptance, improved employment options, higher salary, elevated marriage rates, and greater self-confidence.

Now that you've been working on this for 3 weeks and have experienced some success making changes, can you think of new ways that this lifestyle is beneficial? Have you begun to notice any improvements in your own life? Do you feel better about your relationship with food and your body? Do you feel more self-assured? Do you feel better about your body?

We have discussed the importance of making slight decreases in your caloric intake to achieve a better balance between caloric input and output.

We've also discussed several principles for changing dietary intake, including substituting lower calorie foods for higher calorie foods, starting meals with foods that are high in water content, using smaller portion sizes, and changing your food environment.

Were you able to make the planned adjustment to your intake? Which principles did you use?

What are some of the things that make these types of changes difficult? How did you overcome them (or if you didn't, how could you overcome them in the future)?

Have each participant discuss how the change plan worked last week. If they did not make the behavior change, briefly assess what happened and brainstorm solutions. Let group members provide input to each other.

Apply principles of behavior modification when possible (e.g., making small, observable changes, making the behavior change before participating in an enjoyable activity, reinforcing changes).

Can each of you identify one additional way that you can make your diet healthier? Please review your food record and the handouts you have for ideas.

Go around the room so that each participant can state one additional healthy change to their diet. Continue to encourage small, achievable changes. Again, let group members provide support for each other with regard to future changes.

Are each of you willing to continue these changes in intake for the next 6 months?

Go around the room to get a public commitment to maintaining these changes.

Healthy Exercise Change and Future Exercise Change (15 minutes)

We also talked about the importance of increasing your exercise level to help you achieve a better balance between your intake and output.

We discussed principles that may help you increase your physical activity, including scheduling time for exercise, selected exercise that you enjoy, engaging in incidental exercise, and thinking flexibly about ways to exercise.

Were you able to make the planned changes to your exercise routine? What did you do? Did you use one of the principles? What are some of the things that make these types of changes difficult?

Go around the room and troubleshoot as necessary. If a participant did not complete the behavior change plan, briefly assess what happened and brainstorm solutions. Let group members provide input for each other.

Apply principles of behavior modification when possible, such as rewarding yourself for making the healthy change in your exercise routine.

Can each of you identify one additional way that you can make your exercise routine healthier? Please review your exercise record and the handouts for ideas.

Go around the room so that each participant can state one additional healthy change to their exercise routine. Again, let group members provide support for each other with regard to future changes.

Are each of you willing to continue these changes in intake for the next 6 months? If you don't see a benefit by then, you can stop, but I suspect you will be very happy with the changes! Additionally, continuing an established routine is much easier than initiating one, so you have already done the hardest part.

Relapse Prevention (10 minutes)

Discuss anticipated barriers to continuing these lifestyle changes. Encourage participants to try to identify these obstacles ahead of time so that they will be prepared to deal with them. Having a plan of action will help avoid the common problem of getting permanently off track.

Can you anticipate things that will make it difficult to continue these healthy behaviors? Think about situations that have made past behavior change plans fail. For example, have scheduling difficulties resulting from changing classes from one semester to the next caused problems? For many people, finals are a particularly stressful time when eating and exercise patterns are disrupted (sometimes permanently!). Breakups of relationships are also stressful. In the future, pregnancy and becoming a new mother may make it difficult to continue the healthy eating and exercise changes you've adopted in this course.

Thinking ahead, can you come up with ways to respond to these challenges?

Go around the room so that everyone talks.

We should note that sometimes people "slip" and eat something unhealthy or blow-off a planned workout. Often people use this as an excuse to go back to their old, unhealthy lifestyle. Don't do it!

One skill that people who maintain a healthy weight have is that they "get back on the horse if they fall off." Slips are inevitable—no one is perfect. The trick is to not let the slip lead you to stop all the improvements you are making in your life.

Also, if you have a slip, don't punish yourself. If your plan is that you want to walk 20 minutes everyday and you miss two days, for example, don't try to make yourself walk 60 minutes on the third day; just get back to doing the 20 minutes you are committed to. Or, if you eat more high caloric food than you wanted to on a certain day, don't starve yourself the next day. Just go back to your healthy eating habits the next day. If you stop working out for a week during finals, don't be too hard on yourself, just start up again as soon as you can.

Stay committed to a healthy lifestyle and realize that sometimes you will slip. The important thing is to view these slips as opportunities to learn how to not slip next time. If you view it as a life-long process, you can see that one slip-up is not complete failure.

Emphasize that returning to their routine as quickly as possible is the goal. It is often helpful to troubleshoot where things got off track, but encourage participants to do so with a curious, nonjudgmental approach.

Reasons for Signing Up for this Class (10 minutes)

As the final session comes to a close, it is helpful to get participants to share the reasons they were interested in joining this group.

Are any of you willing to share what made you sign up for this body acceptance class?

Have group members share as much as they are comfortable with.

Have the changes you have made helped you feel better about your body?

Lead this discussion into ways that they can further improve their diet and exercise to approximate their goals.

Home Exercises

■ Instruct group members to e-mail you (and your co-leader) in one week to let you know how their lifestyle alterations are going. Get public commitment from each group member that they will contact you. If necessary, you may send your own e-mails to remind them.

Wrap-Up

Thank you very much for participating in this group. I have been very impressed with your thoughtful comments and participation. It is wonderful that you have been willing to make healthy lifestyle changes to help you achieve a healthier body size and improved body acceptance.

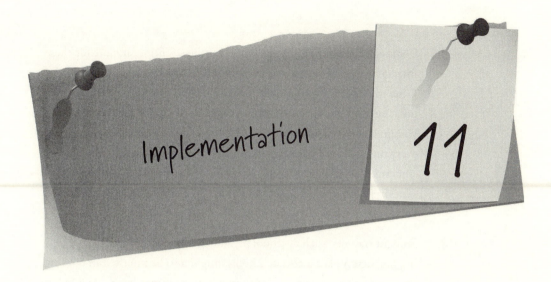

Implementation 11

Over the last decade we have had the opportunity to offer the Body Project and the Healthy Weight interventions to students in numerous high schools and universities. The aim of this final chapter is to share what we have learned about (1) securing approval from school administrators for prevention programs of this nature, (2) successfully recruiting students for these interventions, (3) retaining students in the intervention, and (4) the recruitment and training of group leaders who can deliver the interventions with fidelity. Additionally, we provide resources for additional information on eating disorders and referral to mental health professionals.

Securing Administrative Approval

Many individuals may be interested in offering these body acceptance and eating disorder prevention programs in high schools and universities. Securing administrative approval for such prevention programs should be relatively straightforward for school counselors, nurses, and psychologists who work in the school. In most settings, these individuals will simply need to ask permission to offer prevention programs for students at elevated risk for eating disorders. Informing supervisors that these programs have been found to reduce risk for current and future eating disorder symptoms, reduce risk for future onset of obesity, and result in improved psychosocial functioning (e.g., in-school functioning) in several controlled trials should increase the chances of gaining approval.

Chapter 1 provides greater details about the scientific support for these interventions. It is often useful to point out that offering eating disorder prevention programs may also serve an important public relations purpose for the school. Given the prevalence of eating disorders among young women, it almost certain that there are at least a few students in every high school and university with serious eating disorders. Parents of students with eating disorders are typically relieved to know that prevention programs are in place to reduce the risk that other children will develop eating disorders.

Student trainees, such as school psychology interns and nurses completing practicum placements at schools, might also be intersted in offering these prevention programs. Because it may be somewhat more difficult to secure approval for trainees to facilitate these interventions, it might be necessary to make a more formal presentation regarding the beneficial effects of these interventions in school settings. Again, the material in chapter 1 should provide enough information for such a presentation. It will be particularly important for trainees to note that these interventions have been previously found to be effective when delivered by trainees (e.g., graduate students) and even by individuals who have not yet completed their college degree.

In general, administrators are most receptive to offering these programs when (1) it is demonstrated that research supports a beneficial effect of the intervention for participants, (2) the implementation of these programs do not interfere with regular school activities, and (3) it does not require any additional burden on the school administrative staff.

Participant Recruitment

One of the more challenging aspects of offering these prevention programs is recruiting students who are at elevated risk for eating disorders because of body image concerns. Many prevention interventionists use a schoolwide screening measure to identify female students with body image concerns (i.e., administer a body satisfaction measure to all students). Although this approach is an effective method of identifying students with body image disturbances, we have relied on self-selection to identify students with body image concerns who are interested in a body acceptance intervention. We allow anyone to participate who feels that they have body image concerns without requiring that they are elevated on a particular measure of body dissatisfaction. We took this approach because it does not require us to use a school-wide survey to label students as high risk and because it is easier for school staff. Additionally, with self-selection individuals who do not score above a cut-off are not excluded from participating, even though that they may be interested and feel that they do have body image concerns.

There are several considerations that are helpful in successfully recruiting participants. First, it is critical that potential participants are aware that the program is being offered in their schools. Typically, we send mass mailings out to all female students at a particular school, inviting young women with body image concerns to sign up for a body acceptance class. This is by far the most effective recruitment approach. We often find it useful to send a second mailing two weeks after the first mailing (typically just a postcard). In addition, we have made announcements over the intercom system in high schools during homeroom hours. It is also helpful to ask teachers or professors to announce the program in classes. Furthermore, we also ask the school nurse or counselor to mention the program to individuals who may be appropriate for the intervention. It is often helpful to solicit involvement from community members, parents, community organizations, or school/campus groups (e.g., sororities, clubs) to generate awareness of and interest in the program. We have also relied on using flyers with interesting captions or pictures that capture attention as a means of recruiting participants. Using flyers with rip-off tabs and posting flyers in restroom stalls or other locations where individuals can access the information with some privacy is also useful because body image concerns are often a sensitive topic among adolescents.

A second feature of successful recruitment involves presenting the program as an interesting and fun opportunity for participants. For many individuals, these topics are inherently interesting and provocative, so it is essential to capitalize on this during recruitment. Because many students are already overloaded with school work, it is particularly important to avoid presenting the program as simply another instructional class requiring more work.

Third, participants are more likely to enroll in this program when potential barriers to attendance have been removed. For example, conducting the sessions on the school campus, rather than requiring participants to travel to another location, makes it easier to participate. The timing of the sessions can also affect recruitment. In our experience, the most effective times to hold sessions are immediately after school (generally, within 30 minutes of school dismissal), or at times that do not conflict with college class schedules or compete with popular extracurricular activities (e.g., sorority meetings, band practice). Holding sessions no more than once per week can also help increase attendance and avoid potential scheduling conflicts.

Participant Retention

Once participants have been recruited, a primary goal is retaining students in the intervention. One way of accomplishing this is to create a relaxed atmosphere that facilitates discussion among participants. This often means holding sessions in a conference room or comfortable space where they can face each other, rather than in a classroom. Another key aspect of retention involves reminding participants about the sessions and the home exercises. We recommend contacting participants by phone or e-mail the day before each scheduled session to help improve attendance and to prompt participants to complete and bring their home exercises. Furthermore, participants may be more likely to attend sessions if they feel confident that their personal information will be treated sensitively and confidentially. Group leaders should emphasize the importance of confidentiality in the group. Occasionally, participants discuss personal situations that involve other students or friends outside the group. When doing so, they should be instructed to omit any personal identifying information (e.g., names or detailed descriptions). Additionally, group leaders should refrain from discussing the sessions with colleagues or other school personnel not involved in the intervention. Ensuring that any sensitive information that is disclosed remains confidential promotes group cohesion and trust and encourages continued participation. When offered in a school setting, we recommend that this intervention not be offered if sessions would occur during different semesters or quarters because participants may have to drop out if their course schedule changes or if they starting a new sport or activity half way through the intervention.

Individuals who conduct this intervention as part of a research study and plan to collect data on height and weight or plan to conduct interviews should pay particular attention to how they obtain sensitive data. For example, participants should weighed in a private location, and friends or other group members should not be allowed to be present.

Recruitment and Training of Group Leaders

The recruitment and training of group leaders who can deliver the interventions with fidelity is also an important consideration. As we mentioned previously, research suggests that this program can be delivered successfully by individuals with varying degrees of clinical training, but there are several characteristics that should be considered when selecting group leaders. Experience indicates that the most successful group leaders are those who are enthusiastic and engaging and display a high degree of professionalism while facilitating lively discussion of the material or even incorporating humor into the discussions. Effective group leaders should also understand and embrace the underlying theory behind this intervention. Individuals who have a background in counseling, social work, psychology, or nursing or who are trainees in these areas may be particularly good candidates for group leaders.

Training for group leaders should include several steps. First, group leaders should familiarize themselves with the underlying dissonance theory and background information contained in this manual. It is essential that group leaders carefully read the manual and practice each activity before attempting to lead a group. Group leaders may choose to audio or videotape sessions, with appropriate consent from the participants, to review and gauge the fidelity with which they administer the protocol. This can be of particular use in research studies, wherein independent raters can assess adherence in the taped sessions. We have also found it helpful for novice group leaders to first co-facilitate the group with a more experienced clinician, then take over responsibility for leading the group with the experienced group leader as a cofacilitator, who can provide feedback on the delivery of the intervention.

Delivery of Intervention

The delivery of this intervention will differ slightly depending on the population. Below we discuss some of the main differences that have emerged from conducting this intervention with both high school-age and college-age participants.

When discussing the particular pressures to be thin that group members encounter, group leaders should tailor the discussion to address issues relevant to that population. For example, a common issue among college-age participants surrounds concerns about the "freshman fifteen" (i.e., excess weight that is gained during the first year of college, usually due to poorer eating habits and/or reduced physical activity). However, high school students may be more concerned with looking slim for their school prom or with pressure they receive from athletic coaches to maintain a particular weight.

Another difference between these populations surrounds their social environment. Most high school participants live at home and may encounter substantial pressure to be thin (either intentional or unintentional) from family members. Given that they must function within this family system, it may be necessary to discuss ways in which they can address such issues. Additionally, high school students are not as readily able to modify their food environment, particularly if they are not the primary family member responsible for purchasing groceries or preparing meals.

More generally, it is important to ensure that the discourse is appropriate for the developmental level of the group members. It may be necessary to provide younger participants with more encouragement to discuss the issues addressed in the intervention or to share their personal experiences. Younger participants also tend to require more group management (e.g., when members begin an off-topic discussion), particularly if friends are in the same group. For these reasons, it may be useful to offer separate groups for first- and second-year students and for third- and fourth-year students in high schools.

Eating disorders are serious health conditions that require professional help, and early diagnosis and intervention can improve the chances of recovery. In the event that participants experience significant eating disorder symptoms during the course of the intervention, it is essential that facilitators identify these individuals and refer them to more intensive interventions designed to treat their problems. It is important to keep in mind that this program is intended as a prevention intervention; it is not appropriate for, nor sufficient to treat, individuals with an eating disorder. Below we provide some guidelines regarding when to refer participants to treatment and where to find information about eating disorders and appropriate referral sources.

Although the *DSM-IV-TR* outlines formal guidelines for the diagnosis of eating disorders, these behaviors exist on a continuum. Clearly, any individual who meets the diagnostic criteria for an eating disorder should be identified and referred to treatment. However, even individuals who do not meet the full criteria for an eating disorder may experience significant distress and engage in behaviors that put their physical and psychological health at risk. For example, recent research suggests that individuals who engage in binge eating (defined as an episode in which the person consumes an objectively large amount of food accompanied by a sense of loss of control) an average of once a week do not differ from those who binge more often (Le Grange et al., 2006). Therefore, those who meet all other criteria for bulimia nervosa or binge eating disorder but fail to meet the frequency or duration requirement for binge eating may be viewed as subthreshhold cases that warrant referral for treatment. Similarly, individuals who meet all criteria for anorexia nervosa but whose weight is marginally above the threshold or who do not meet the amenorrhea requirement should be referred. Other cases that should be referred for more intensive intervention include individuals who engage in repeated purging or other inappropriate compensatory behavior in the absence of objective binge episodes, or repeated chewing and spitting out large amounts of food without swallowing.

The following resources may be helpful in providing additional information about eating disorders and in locating appropriate referrals.

American Psychological Association
750 1st Street, NE
Washington, DC 20002-4242
(202) 336-5510
www.apa.org

Association for Behavior and Cognitive Therapy
305 7th Avenue, 16th Floor, New York, NY 10001
(212) 647-1890; Fax: (212) 647-1865
www.aabt.org

American Psychiatric Association
1000 Wilson Boulevard, Suite 1825
Arlington, VA 22209
(703) 907-7300
www.healthyminds.org

National Eating Disorders Association
603 Stewart Street, Suite 803
Seattle, WA 98101
(206) 382-3587; toll-free: 1-800-931-2237
www.nationaleatingdisorders.org

National Association of Anorexia and Associated Disorders
P.O. Box 7
Highland Park, IL 60035
(847) 831-3438
www.anad.org

Academy for Eating Disorders
6728 Old McLean Village Drive
McLean, VA 22101
(703) 556-9222
www.aedweb.org

National Institute of Mental Health
6001 Executive Boulevard
Room 8184, MSC 9663
Bethesda, MD 20892
(301) 443-4513

www.nimh.nih.gov
NIMH Mental Health Services Locator:
   www.mentalhealth.samhsa.gov/databases/

National Mental Health Association
1021 Prince Street
Alexandria, VA 22314-2971
(703) 684-7722
www.nmha.org

Appendix

Facilitator Fact Sheet

A. Fashion magazines (according to a former fashion magazine editor and the International Conference on Eating Disorders)

    1. Function of a fashion magazine: To convince women that something is wrong with them (e.g., hair, body, sex life) so that advertisers can sell their products to fix the perceived problem. The more anxious they make you, the more likely you will buy the magazine and the larger their readership, which increases advertising sales.

        a. How they convince you something is wrong

            ■ Lead articles: A Pulitzer Prize-winning article on eating disorders or ovarian cancer is not going to increase advertising sales, but an article with a title like "You never knew what your butt looked like from the rear! Strategies for a better behind" will.

            ■ Idealized images: Photographs are digitally enhanced, models have make up professionally applied, clothes are pinned, and so on.

        b. At this editor's magazine, many of the key staff had eating disorders due to a culture of disordered eating and weight/shape attitudes.

            ■ They couldn't bring food into the office because it was too upsetting for some staff.

            ■ One woman brought a scale to work and moved the scale around the bathroom floor until she got an acceptable weight.

B. Advertising strategies
  1. Physical tactics
     a. Bras are stuffed with pads to fill out the front of a dress that is too loose.
     b. Padded underwear is also used to fill out the back of a dress.
     c. Duct tape is often used to tape breasts together to create cleavage.
     d. Girdles are used to squeeze the models into a dress sample size that is too small.
     e. Excess flesh is duct-taped in the back for a front-angle photograph depicting a taut, streamlined, wrinkle-free body. Models can be taped from the front for a rear or side-angle photograph showing tight, firm hips, bottoms, legs, and arms.
     f. Heavy clamps are used to cinch clothing in and weigh it down to create an illusion of the perfect fit.
     g. Often, body doubles are used in films, TV commercials, and magazine advertising.
  2. Computer tactics
     a. Once a photo shoot is complete, images are altered even further through a process called reimaging. By scanning the photograph into a computer, the image can be altered in thousands of ways. Almost every magazine uses computer reimaging in some way:
        ■ Complexion is cleaned up, eye lines are softened, chins, thighs. and stomachs are trimmed, and neck lines are removed.
        ■ Some of the pictures of the models in magazines do not really exist. The pictures are computer-modified compilations of different body parts.
        ■ The television news show *20/20* aired a story of a photo shoot of supermodel Cindy Crawford. Two hours were spent digitally editing and airbrushing her face and body.

C. Fashion models versus average women
1. The average American woman is 5′4″ tall and weighs 140 pounds. The average American model is 5′11″ tall and weighs 117 pounds.
   a. The average American woman wears a size 12 to 14.
   b. Marilyn Monroe, the Hollywood goddess, wore a size 12.
2. Most fashion models are thinner than 98% of American women (Smolak, 1996).
   a. Twenty years ago, models weighed 8% less than the average woman. Today they weigh 23% less, and many fall into an anorexic weight range.
   b. Kate Moss is 5′7″ and weighs 95 pounds. That is 30% below ideal body weight. Supermodels Niki Taylor and Elle Macpherson also meet the body mass index criteria for anorexia.
3. Only 5% of women have the body type (tall, genetically thin, broad-shouldered, narrow-hipped, long-legged and usually small-breasted) seen in almost all advertising. (When the models have large breasts, they've almost always had breast implants.)

D. Dieting, exercise, and self-image
1. Americans spend more than $40 billion on dieting and diet-related products each year (Smolak, 1996).
   a. A study of mass media magazines discovered that women's magazines had 10.5 times more advertisements and articles promoting weight loss than men's magazines did (Guillen & Barr, 1994).
   b. Ninety-five percent of enrollees in weight loss programs are women, even though the sexes are overweight in equal proportions.
   c. Women who have a history of chronic yo-yo dieting can decrease their overall lifespan of up to 20%.
2. In 1995, before television was first introduced to Fiji, there were no cases of eating disorders. Sixty-five adolescent school girls were followed over 3 years:
   a. After the introduction of British and American television, 12.7% of the girls had developed severe eating disorder symptoms after 1 month and 29.2% after 3 years.

■ Self-induced vomiting as a weight control mechanism went from 0% in 1995 to 11.3% by 1998.

3. Celebrities work out from 90 minutes to up to 6–7 hours a day.
    a. P. Diddy has a personal trainer that he pays $500,000 a year (VH-1).
    b. Usher does 1000 crunches per day plus daily "forty minutes funk" (stretching and cardio) and strength training.
    c. Hilary Swank, in preparing for *Million Dollar Baby*, exercised 4.5 hours per day, six days per week (from Oprah online).

4. A study in 1995 found that after just 3 minutes spent looking at models in a fashion magazine, 70% of women reported feeling depressed, guilty, and ashamed of their bodies.

5. A 1996 study found that the amount of time an adolescent watches soap operas, movies, and music videos is associated with their degree of body dissatisfaction and desire to be thin (Tiggemann & Pickering, 1996).

6. If shop mannequins were real women, they would be too thin to menstruate and bear children.
    a. Rintala & Mustajoki (1992) reported in the *British Medical Journal* that store mannequins do not have enough body fat to menstruate. The researchers visited clothing stores, and based on measurements of the mannequins calculated the percentage body fat that a woman the shape of a mannequin would carry. In direct contradiction to the slim, healthy, and fertile physique that mannequins seek to portray and inflict on women, the finding of the study was that, overwhelmingly, shop mannequins, if they were people, would be infertile.
    b. Clothing on mannequins is pinned, so clothes would never look the same on a real person unless it was pinned exactly perfect.

7. Women naturally carry fat on their hips and thighs—it is vital for fertility, prevention of osteoporosis, healthy skin, eyes, hair, and teeth.

8. The National Weight Loss Registry, run by the universities of Pittsburgh and Colorado, tracks those that have achieved significant, long-term weight loss and has documented that not

one person has been successful by eliminating or severely restricting one of the macronutrients (protein, carbohydrate and fat).

a. Long-term weight loss typically associated with low-fat, low calorie maintenance diet along with 1 hour of moderate exercise most days per week.

9. In the study, "Exposure to the mass media and weight concerns among girls" by Field, Cheung, Wolf, Herzog, Gortmaker, & Colditz (1999), the authors used a cross-sectional survey of 548 girls in fifth grade through twelfth grade to assess influence of the media on weight concerns, weight control behaviors and perceptions of body weight and shape.

a. A majority of girls (59%) reported dissatisfaction with their body shape, and 66% expressed the desire to lose weight; the prevalence of overweight in this study was 29%.

b. Girls were asked about their frequency of reading women's fashion magazines. Some 69% reported that appearance of models in the magazines influenced their image of a perfect female body, and 47% desired to lose weight because of the magazine pictures.

References

Agras, W. S., Walsh, B. T., Fairburn, C. G., Wilson, G. T., & Kraemer, H. C. (2000). A multicenter comparison of cognitive-behavioral therapy and interpersonal therapy for bulimia nervosa. *Archives of General Psychiatry, 57,* 459–466.

American Psychiatric Association (2000). *Diagnostic and statistical manual of mental disorders* (4th ed., text revision).Washington, DC: Author.

American Psychological Association Task Force on Psychological Intervention Guidelines. (1995). *Template for developing guidelines: Interventions for mental disorders and psychological aspects of physical disorders.* Washington, DC: American Psychological Association.

Austin, S. B. (2001). Population-based prevention of eating disorders: An application of the Rose prevention model. *Preventive Medicine, 32,* 268–283.

Bathalon, G. P., Tucker, K. L., Hays, N. P., Vinken, A. G., Greenberg, A. S. McCrory, M. A., et al. (2000). Psychological measures of eating behavior and the accuracy of 3 common dietary assessment methods in healthy postmenopausal women. *American Journal of Clinical Nutrition, 71,* 739–745.

Bearman, S. K., Stice, E., & Chase, A. (2003). Effects of body dissatisfaction on depressive and bulimic symptoms: A longitudinal experiment. *Behavior Therapy, 34,* 277–293.

Becker, C. B., Ciao, A. C., Smith, L. M., Bell, J. L., Hemberger, L. J., & Franco, A. (2005). *Peer-led eating disorders prevention in sorority members: Cognitive dissonance versus media psychoeducation.* Paper presented at the 2005 International Conference on Eating Disorders, Montreal, Canada.

Becker, C. B., Jilka, K., & Polvere, L. (2002). *Cognitive dissonance vs. media psychoeducation: A pilot study of eating disorder prevention in sorority members.* Paper presented at the Association for the Advancement of Behavior Therapy, Reno, NV.

Becker, C. B., Smith, L., & Ciao, A. C. (2005). Reducing eating disorder risk factors in sorority members: A randomized trial. *Behavior Therapy, 36,* 245–254.

Becker, C. B., Smith, L., & Ciao, A. C. (2006). Peer-facilitated eating disorder prevention: A randomized effectiveness trial of cognitive dissonance and media advocacy. *Journal of Counseling Psychology, 53*(4), 550–555.

Berscheid, E., Walster, E., & Bohrnstedt, G. (1973). The happy American body: A survey report. *Psychology Today, 7,* 119–131.

Bohon, E., Muscatell, K., Burton, E., & Stice, E. (2005). Maintenance factors for persistence of bulimic pathology: A community-based natural history study. Poster presented at the annual meeting of the Eating Disorder Research Society, Toronto, Canada.

Burton, E., & Stice, E. (2006). Evaluation of a healthy-weight treatment program for bulimia nervosa: A preliminary randomized trial. *Behaviour Research & Therapy, 44,* 1727–1738.

Burton, E. M., Stice, E., Bearman, S. K., & Rohde, P. (in press). An experimental test of the affect-regulation model of bulimic symptoms and substance use: An affective intervention. *International Journal of Eating Disorders.*

Cachelin, F. M., Striegel-Moore, R. H., Elder, K. A., Pike, K. M., Wilfley, D. E., & Fairburn, C. G. (1999). Natural course of a community sample of women with binge eating disorder. *International Journal of Eating Disorders, 25*(1), 45–54.

Calle, E. F., Thun, M. J., Petrelli, J. M., Rodriguez, C., & Heath, C. W. (1999). Body mass index and mortality in a prospective cohort of U.S. adults. *New England Journal of Medicine, 341,* 1097–1105.

Capaldi, D. M., & Stoolmiller, M. (1999). Co-occurrence of conduct problems and depressive symptoms in early adolescent boys: III. Prediction to young-adult adjustment. *Development and Psychopathology, 11*(1), 59–84.

Cattarin, J. A., & Thompson, J. K. (1994). A three-year longitudinal study of body image, eating disturbance, and general psychological functioning in adolescent females. *Eating Disorders, 2*(2), 114–125.

Clarke, G. N., Hawkins, W., Murphy, M., Sheeber, L. (1993). School-based primary prevention of depressive symptomatology in adolescents: Findings from two studies. *Journal of Adolescent Research, 8,* 183–204.

Coie, J., Watt, N., West, S., Hawkins, D., Asarnow, J., Markman, H., Ramey, S., Shore, M., & Long, B. (1993). The science of prevention:

A conceptual framework and some directions for a national research program. *American Psychologist, 48,* 1013–1022.

Cooley, E., & Toray, T. (2001). Body image and personality predictors of eating disorder symptoms during the college years. *International Journal of Eating Disorders, 30*(1), 28–36,

Dietz, W. H. (2004). Overweight in childhood and adolescence. *New England Journal of Medicine, 350,* 885–857.

Fairburn, C. G., & Cooper, Z. (1993). The eating disorder examination (12th ed.). In C. Fairburn & G. Wilson (Eds.), *Binge eating: Nature, assessment, and treatment* (pp. 317–360). New York: Guilford.

Fairburn, C. G., Cooper, Z., Doll, H., Norman, P., & O'Connor, M. (2000). The natural course of bulimia nervosa and binge eating disorder in young women. *Archives of General Psychiatry, 57*(7), 659–665.

Favaro, A., Ferrara, S., & Santonastaso, P. (2003). The spectrum of eating disorders in young women: A prevalence study in a general population sample. *Psychosomatic Medicine, 65*(4), 701–708.

Festinger, L. (1957). *A Theory of Cognitive Dissonance.* Stanford: Stanford University Press.

Field, A. E., Camargo, C. A., Taylor, C. B., Berkey, C. S., & Colditz, G. A. (1999). Relation of peer and media influences to the development of purging behaviors among preadolescent and adolescent girls. Archives of Pediatric *Adolescent Medicine, 153,* 1184–1189.

Field, A. E., Camargo, C. A., Taylor, C. B., Berkey, C. S., Roberts, S. B., & Colditz, G. A. (2001). Peer-parent, and media influences on the development of weight concerns and frequent dieting among preadolescent and adolescent girls and boys. *Pediatrics, 107*(1), 54–60.

Flegal, K. M., Graubard, B. I., Williamson, D. F., & Gail, M. H. (2005). Excess deaths associated with underweight, overweight, and obesity. *Journal of the American Medical Association, 293,* 1861–1867.

Gotlib, I. H., Lewinsohn, P. M., & Seeley, J. R. (1998). Consequences of depression during adolescence: Marital status and marital functioning in early adulthood . *Journal of Abnormal Psychology. 107*(4), 686–690.

Green, M., Scott, N., Diyankova, I., Gasser, C., & Pederson, E. (2005). Eating disorder prevention: An experimental comparison of high level dissonance, low level dissonance, and no-treatment control. *Eating Disorders, 13,* 157–170.

Grilo, C. M., Sanislow, C. A., Shea, M. T., Skodol, A. E., Stout, R. L., Pagano, M. E., et al. (2003). The natural course of bulimia nervosa and eating disorder not otherwise specified is not influenced by personality disorders. *International Journal of Eating Disorders, 34*(3), 319–330.

Groesz, L. M., & Stice, E. (2007). An experimental test of the effects of dieting on bulimic symptoms: The impact of eating episode frequency. *Behaviour Research and Therapy, 45,* 49–62.

Hedley, A. A., Ogden, C. L., Johnson, C. L., Carroll, M. D., Curtin, L. R., & Flegal, K. M. (2004). Prevalence of overweight and obesity among U.S. children, adolescents, and adults, 1999–2000. *Journal of the American Medical Association, 291,* 2847–2850.

Hoagwood, K., Hibbs, E., Brent, D., & Jensen, P. (1995). Introduction to the special section: Efficacy and effectiveness in studies of child and adolescent psychotherapy. *Journal of Consulting and Clinical Psychology, 63,* 683–687.

Hoek, H. W., & van Hoeken, D. (2003). Review of the prevalence and incidence of eating disorders. *International Journal of Eating Disorders, 34*(4), 383–396.

Johnson, J. G., Cohen, P., Kasen, S., & Brook, J. S. (2002). Eating disorders during adolescence and the risk for physical and mental disorders during early adulthood. *Archives of General Psychiatry. 59,* 545–552.

Keel, P. K., Dorer, J. Eddy, K. T., Franko, D., Charatan, D. L., Herzog, D. B., et al. (2003). Predictors of mortality in eating disorders. *Archives of General Psychiatry, 60*(2), 179–183.

Killen, J. D., Taylor, C. B., Hammer, L., Litt, I., Wilson, D. M., Rich, T., et al., (1993). An attempt to modify unhealthful eating attitudes and weight regulation practices of young adolescent girls. *International Journal of Eating Disorders, 13,* 369–384.

Killen, J. D., Taylor, C. B., Hayward, C., Haydel, K. F., Wilson, D. M., Hammer, L., Kraemer, H., Blair-Greiner, A., & Strachowski, D. (1996). Weight concerns influence the development of eating disorders: A 4-year prospective study. *Journal of Consulting and Clinical Psychology, 64,* 936–940.

Killen, J. D., Taylor, C. B., Hayward, C., Wilson, D. M., Haydel, K. F., Hammer, L. D., et al. (1994). Pursuit of thinness and onset of eating disorder symptoms in a community sample of adolescent girls: A three-year prospective analysis. *International Journal of Eating Disorders, 16*(3), 227–238.

Kjelsas, E. Bjornstrom, C., & Gotestam, K. G. (2004). Prevalence of eating disorders in female and male adolescents (14–15 years). *Eating Behaviors, 5*(1), 13–25.

Larimer, M. E., & Cronce, J. M. (2002). Identification, prevention, and treatment: A review of individual-focused strategies to reduce problematic alcohol consumption by college students. *Journal of Studies on Alcohol, 14,* 148–163.

Leake, R., Friend, R., & Wadhwa, N. (1999). Improving adjustment of chronic illness through strategic self-presentation: An experimental study on a renal dialysis unit. *Health Psychology, 18,* 54–62.

Leippe, M. R. (1994). Generalization of dissonance reduction: Decreasing prejudice through induced compliance. *Journal of Personality and Social Psychology, 67,* 395–413.

Levine, M. D., Marcus, M. D., & Moulton, P. (1996). Exercise in the treatment of binge eating disorder. *International Journal of Eating Disorders, 19,* 171–177.

Levine, M.P. & Smolak, L. (2006). The prevention of eating problems and eating disorder: Theory, research, and practice. Mahwah, NJ: Erlbaum Associates.

Levine, M. P. & Smolak, L. (2001). Primary prevention of body image disturbances and disordered eating in childhood and early adolescence. In J. K. Thompson & L. Smolak (eds.) *Body image, eating disorders, and obesity in youth: Assessment, prevention and treatment* (pp. 237–260). American Psychological Association: Washington DC.

Lewinsohn, P. M., Hops, H., Roberts, R. E., Seeley, J. R., & Andrews, J. A. (1993). Adolescent psychopathology: I. Prevalence and incidence of depression and other DSM-III-R disorders in high school students. *Journal of Abnormal Psychology, 102*(1), 133–144.

Lewinsohn, P. M., Solomon, A., Seeley, J. R., & Zeiss, A. (2000). Clinical implications of "subthreshold"' depressive symptoms. *Journal of Abnormal Psychology. 109*(2), 345–351.

Lewinsohn, P. M., Striegel-Moore, R. H., & Seeley, J. R. (2000). Epidemiology and natural course of eating disorders in young women from adolescence to young adulthood. *Journal of the American Academy of Child and Adolescent Psychiatry, 39,* 1284–1292.

Magarey, A. M., Daniels, L. A., Boulton, T. J., & Cockington, R. A. (2003). Predicting obesity in early adulthood from childhood and parental obesity. *International Journal of Obesity and Related Metabolic Disorders, 27,* 505–513.

Mann, J. M., Tarantola, D. J., & Netter, T. W. (1992). *AIDS in the world.* Cambridge, MA: Harvard University Press.

Martin, C. K., Williamson, D. A., Geiselman, P. J., Walden, H., Smeets, M., Morales, S., & Redman, S. (2005). Consistency of food intake over four eating sessions in the laboratory. *Eating Behaviors, 6,* 365–372.

Matusek, J. A., Wendt, S. J., & Wiseman, C. V. (2004). Dissonance thin-ideal and didactic healthy behavior eating disorder prevention programs: Results from a controlled trial. *International Journal of Eating Disorders, 36,* 376–388.

McKnight Investigators (2003). Risk factors for the onset of eating disorders in adolescent girls: Results of the McKnight longitudinal risk factor study. *American Journal of Psychiatry, 160*(2), 248–254.

McVey, G. L., Lieberman, M., Voorberg, N., Wardrope, D., & Blackmore, E. (2003). School-based peer support groups: A new approach to the prevention of disordered eating. *Eating Disorders, 11,* 169–185.

McVey, G. L., Lieberman, M., Voorberg, N., Wardrope, D., Blackmore, E. & Tweed, S. (2003). Replication of a peer support program designed to prevent disordered eating: Is life skills approach sufficient for all middle school students? *Eating Disorders, 11,* 187–195.

Miller, W. R. (1983). Motivational interviewing with problem drinkers. *Behavioral Psychotherapy, 11,* 147–172.

Neumark-Sztainer, D., Butler, R., & Palti, H. (1995). Eating disturbances among adolescent girls: Evaluation of a school-based primary prevention program. *Journal of Nutritional Education, 27,* 24–31.

Newman, D. L., Moffitt, T. E., Caspi, A., Magdol, L., Silva, P. A., & Stanton, W. R. (1996). Psychiatric disorder in a birth cohort young adults prevalence, comorbidity, clinical significance, and new case incidence from ages 11 to 21. *Journal of Consulting and Clinical Psychology, 64,* 552–562.

Nolen-Hoeksema, S., Girgus, J. S., & Seligman, M. E. P. (1992). Predictors and consequences of childhood depressive symptoms: A 5-year longitudinal study. *Journal of Abnormal Psychology, 101*(3), 405–422.

Ogden, C. L., Flegal, K. M., Carroll, M. D., & Johnson, C. L. (2002). Prevalence and trends in overweight among US children and adolescents, 1999–2000. *Journal of the American Medical Association, 288,* 1728–1732.

Pietrobelli, A., Faith, M. S., Allison, D. B., Gallagher, D., Chiumello, G., & Heymsfield, S. (1998). Body mass index as a measure of adiposity among children and adolescents: A validation study. *Journal of Pediatrics, 132,* 204–210.

Presnell, K., & Stice, E. (2003). An experimental test of the effect of weight-loss dieting on bulimic pathology: Tipping the scales in a different direction. *Journal of Abnormal Psychology, 112,* 166–170.

Roehrig, M., Thompson, J. K., Brannick, M., & van den Berg, P. (2006). Dissonance-based eating disorder prevention program: A preliminary

dismantling investigation. *International Journal of Eating Disorders,*
39, 1–10.

Smolak, L., Levine, M., & Schermer, F. (1998). A controlled evaluation of
an elementary school primary prevention program for eating problems. *Journal of Psychosomatic Research, 44,* 339–353.

Stewart, D. A., Carter, J. C., Drinkwater, J., Hainsworth, J., & Fairburn,
C. G. (2001). Modification of eating attitudes and behavior in adolescent girls: A controlled study. *International Journal of Eating Disorders, 29,* 107–118.

Stice, E. (2001). A prospective test of the dual pathway model of bulimic
pathology: Mediating effects of dieting and negative affect. *Journal of
Abnormal Psychology, 110,* 124–135.

Stice, E., Presnell, K., & Spangler, D. (2002). Risk factors for binge eating
onset in adolescent girls: A 2-year prospective investigation. *Health
Psychology, 21,* 131–138.

Stice, E., & Agras, W. S. (1998). Predicting onset and cessation of bulimic
behaviors during adolescence: A longitudinal grouping analyses. *Behavior Therapy, 29,* 257–276.

Stice, E., Cameron, R., Killen, J. D., Hayward, C., & Taylor, C. B. (1999).
Naturalistic weight reduction efforts prospectively predict growth in
relative weight and onset of obesity among female adolescents. *Journal of Consulting and Clinical Psychology, 67,* 967–974.

Stice, E., Chase, A., Stormer, & Appel, A. (2001). A raondomized trial of
a dissonance-based eating disorder prevention program. *International
Journal of Eating Disorders, 29,* 247–262.

Stice, E., Fisher, M., & Martinez, E. (2004). Eating disorder diagnostic
scale: Additional evidence of reliability and validity. *Psychological Assessment, 16,* 60–71.

Stice, E., Fisher, M., & Lowe, M. R. (2004). Are dietary restraint scales
valid measures of acute dietary restriction? Unobtrusive observational
data suggest not. *Psychological Assessment, 16,* 51–59.

Stice, E., Hayward, C., Cameron, R. P., Killen, J. D., & Taylor, C. B.
(2000). Body-image and eating disturbances predict onset of depression among female adolescents: A longitudinal study. *Journal of Abnormal Psychology, 109*(3), 438–444.

Stice, E., Killen, J.D., Hayward, C. & Taylor, C.B. (1998). Age of onset
for binge eating and purging during adolescence: A four-year survival
analysis. *Journal of Abnormal Psychology, 107,* 671–675.

Stice, E., Mazotti, L., Weibel, D., & Agras, W. S. (2000). Dissonance prevention program decreases thin-ideal internalization, body dissatisfac-

tion, dieting, negative affect, and bulimic symptoms: A preliminary experiment. *International Journal of Eating Disorders, 27,* 206–217.

Stice, E., Presnell, K., Gau, J., & Shaw, H. (2006). Testing mediators of intervention effects in randomized controlled trials: An evaluation of two eating disorder prevention programs. *Journal of Consulting and Clinical Psychology.*

Stice, E. & Shaw, H. (2004). Eating disorder prevention programs: A meta-analytic review. *Psychological Bulletin, 130,* 206–227.

Stice, E., Shaw, H., Burton, E., & Wade, E. (2006). Dissonance and healthy weight eating disorder prevention programs: A randomized efficacy trial. *Journal of Consulting and Clinical Psychology, 74,* 263–275.

Stice, E., Shaw, H., & Marti, C. N. (2006). A meta-analytic review of obesity prevention programs for children and adolescents: The skinny on interventions that work. *Psychological Bulletin, 132,* 667–691.

Stice, E., Telch, C. F., & Rizvi, S. L. (2000). Development and validation of the Eating Disorder Diagnostic Scale: A brief self-report measure for anorexia, bulimia, and binge eating disorder. *Psychological Assessment, 12,* 123–131.

Stice, E., Trost, A., & Chase, A. (2003). Healthy weight control and dissonance-based eating disorder prevention programs: Results from a controlled trial. *International Journal of Eating Disorders, 33,* 10–21.

Stone, J., Aronson, E., Craing, A. L., Winslow, M. P., & Fried, C. B. (1994). Inducing hypocrisy as a means of encouraging young adults to use condoms. *Personality and Social Psychology Bulletin, 20,* 116–128.

Story, M. (1999). School-based approaches for preventing and treating obesity. *International Journal of Obesity and Related Metabolic Disorders, 23,* S43–51.

Striegel-Moore, R. H., Seeley, J. R., & Lewinsohn, P. M. (2003). Psychosocial adjustment in young adulthood of women who experienced an eating disorder during adolescence. *Journal of the American Academy of Child & Adolescent Psychiatry, 42*(5), 587–593.

Strober, M., Freeman, R., & Morrell, W. (1997). The long-term course of severe anorexia nervosa in adolescents: Survival analysis of recovery, relapse, and outcome predictors over 10–15 years in a prospective study. *International Journal of Eating Disorders, 22*(4), 339–360.

Sysko, R., Walsh, T. B., Schebendach, J., & Wilson, G. T. (2005). Eating behaviors among women with anorexia nervosa. *American Journal of Clinical Nutrition, 82,* 296–301.

Thompson, J. K., Heinberg, L. J., Altabe, M., & Tantleff-Dunn, S. (1999). *Exacting beauty: Theory, assessment, and treatment of body image disturbance.* Washington, DC: American Psychological Association.

van Strien, T., Frijters, J. E., van Staveren, W. A., Defares, P. B., & Deurenberg, P. (1986). The predictive validity of the Dutch Restrained Eating Scale. *International Journal of Eating Disorders, 5,* 747–755.

Vogeltanz-Holm, N. D., Wonderlich, S. A., Lewis, B. A., Wilsnack, S. C., Harris, T. R., Wilsnack, R. W., & Kristjanson, A. F. (2000). Longitudinal predictors of binge eating, intense dieting, and weight concerns in a national sample of women. *Behavior Therapy, 31,* 221–235.

Wadden, T. A., Foster, G. D., & Letizia, K. A. (1992). Response of obese binge eaters to treatment by behavior therapy combined with very-low-calorie diet. *Journal of Consulting and Clinical Psychology, 60,* 808–811.

Watson, D., & Clark, L. A. (1992). Affects separable and inseparable: On the hierarchical arrangement of the negative affects. *Journal of Personality and Social Psychology, 62,* 489–505.

Wertheim, E. H., Koerner, J., & Paxton, S. J. (2001). Longitudinal predictors of restrictive eating and bulimic tendencies in three different age groups of adolescent girls. *Journal of Youth and Adolescence, 31,* 69–81.

Wilfley, D. E., Welch, R. R., Stein, R. I., Spurrell, E. B., Cohen, L. R., Saelens, B. E., et al. (2002). A randomized comparison of group cognitive-behavioral therapy and group interpersonal psychotherapy for the treatment of overweight individuals with binge-eating disorder. *Archives of General Psychiatry, 59*(8), 713–721.

Wilson, G. T., Becker, C. B., & Heffernan, K. (2003). Eating Disorders. In E. J. Mash, & R. A. Barkley (Eds.), *Child Psychopathology* (2nd ed., p. 687–715). New York: Guilford.

Wiseman, C. V., Sunday, S. R., Bortolotti, F., & Halmi, K. A. (2004). Primary prevention of eating disorders through attitudinal change: A two country comparison. *Eating Disorders, 12,* 241–250.

Woodside, D. B., Garfinkel, P. E., Lin, E., Goehring, P., Kaplan, A. S., Goldbloom, D. S., et al. (2001). Comparisons of men with full or partial eating disorders, men without eating disorders, and women with eating disorders in the community. *American Journal of Psychiatry, 158*(4), 570–574.

Eric Stice, PhD, is currently a Senior Research Scientist at Oregon Research Institute and the University of Texas at Austin and maintains active research laboratories at both institutions. He completed his undergraduate studies at the University of Oregon, his graduate studies at Arizona State University, his clinical internship at the University of California, San Diego, and his post-doctoral training at Stanford University. After receiving early tenure at the University of Texas at Austin, he transitioned into research scientist positions to that he could devote all of his time to research. One objective of his program of research is to identify risk factors that predict future onset of eating disorders, obesity, and depression, with the goal of refining etiologic theories for these conditions. He has recently begun using brain imaging to elucidate structural and functional neurological factors that may increase risk for these disturbances. A second objective of his research is to develop and evaluate prevention programs for eating disorders, obesity, and depression that are based on the findings from risk factor studies. His research program has been funded by generous grants from the National Institute of Mental Health, the National Institute of Diabetes and Digestive and Kidney Diseases, and the Hogg Foundation for Mental Health. He has published more than 100 scientific articles, meta-analytic reviews, and book chapters to date.

Katherine Presnell, PhD, received her degree in clinical psychology from the University of Texas at Austin in 2005. She completed a clinical internship in health psychology at Duke University Medical Center, specializing in the treatment of eating disorders and obesity. Currently, she is an Assistant Professor in the Department of Psychology at Southern Methodist University (SMU) in Dallas, Texas, and Director of the Weight and Eating Disorders Research Program at SMU. Her program of research focuses on improving our understanding of sociocultural, psychological, and behavioral factors that contribute to both eating disorders and obesity. The emphasis of her current research is on examining the relationship among dieting, weight regulation, and disordered eating, as well as the functional aspects of eating. A second emphasis is the application of this research to the development of prevention programs that reduce risk factors for these disorders and facilitate long-term healthy weight management. Additional research interests include exploring the relationship between emotions and eating. She has published numerous scientific articles in peer-reviewed journals, and her research has been recognized by the Association for Cognitive and Behavioral Therapies.